TALKING WITH THE NEW BUSINESS DRAGONS

D1414669

All love to Isla Elisabeth Petrie born 25th May 2013

To Will, John and Emily
from YingShi

For a complete list of Management Books 2000 titles
visit our website on http://www.mb2000.com

TALKING WITH THE NEW BUSINESS DRAGONS

2nd edition

The fast track to trading successfully

with China

Melville Petrie

Yingshi Helsby

2000

Copyright © Melville Petrie and Yingshi Helsby 2013

All rights reserved. No part of this publication may be reproduced, stored in a retrieval system, or transmitted in any form or by any means, electronic, mechanical, photocopying, recording or otherwise, without the prior permission of the publishers.

The Authors assert their moral rights to be identified as the Authors of the work in relation to all such rights as are granted by the Authors to the Publisher under the terms and conditions of this agreement and in accordance with Copyright, Designs and Patents Act of 1988.

First edition published in 2005 by Management Books 2000 Ltd

This new edition published in 2013 by Management Books 2000 Ltd
36 Western Road
Oxford OX1 4LG
Tel: 0044 (0) 1865 600738
Email: info@mb2000.com
Web: www.mb2000.com

This book is sold subject to the condition that it shall not, by way of trade or otherwise, be lent, resold, hired out, or otherwise circulated without the publisher's prior consent in any form of binding or cover other than that in which it is published and without a similar condition including this condition being imposed upon the subsequent purchaser.

British Library Cataloguing in Publication Data is available

ISBN 9781852527211

CONTENTS

FOREWORD

This revised and refreshed edition of *Talking with the New Business Dragons* remains an outstanding and thoughtful guide to doing business with China. These days you cannot succeed in business globally without in one way or another running up against China which has become a vital trading partner as well as the world's second largest economy. The Chinese are rightly immensely proud of who they are and what they have achieved. Good advice on how best to deal with the gap in cultures which still prevails despite ostensible similarities is simply invaluable. *Talking with the New Business Dragons* provides essential insights into the changing China business environment, its people and how to trade and do business successfully.

Lord Powell of Bayswater KCMG

1

INTRODUCTION TO THE SECOND EDITION

It is only seven years since I wrote the first edition of this handbook but such is the pace of industrial and cultural change in China that whilst most of the tenets remain valid, the Middle Kingdom's outward visage has changed again. Always in competition with its fellow behemothian state, India, she held a stunningly well-managed Olympic Games basking in the glory of acceptance into the global community. India, a much more open society, made a much less certain attempt at the Commonwealth Games – China saw her opportunity to impress the world as a critical undertaking and no obstacle was too great to prevent its consummation. There was social disruption, there was strategic planning on an immense scale, there was such pride in its success that the nation and the diaspora felt deep and genuine pride not only in the glorious opening ceremonies but also in the international recognition of stage management and athleticism.

This is all a long way from the reverence of Chairman Mao's Communism, the events in Tiananmen Square in 1989 and the press coverage of alcohol-soaked Uighur Muslim separatists on open trucks that I drew attention to a few years back. All these influences are still however at work in Chinese society. They remain confusing to outsiders but still western corporations proudly present corporate timepieces to their Chinese counterparts as if it were the first time that business was being done with China.

So, from the business perspective, although China appears to have become more westernised, it remains impenetrable to many. That is not difficult to fathom as she has changed herself. No longer is China content to bask in the sun as the low-cost workshop of the world. Margins are being squeezed as USA and China joust over the value of the Renminbi – the People's Money. There is concern over China's vast foreign currency reserves. There is pride on China's part at keeping western economies afloat during the banking crisis. Nor has the West's previous dismissal of Chinese banking as inherently baseless gone unnoticed. The whole game has changed as China buys up foreign businesses such as IBM and Rover and the same corporations eye up GM. The City of London took a deep breath when the Head of the Bank of China called on his counterpart in the Bank of England at the start of the downturn and announced that not only was he about to make the Renminbi tradable currency in UK with bank accounts available in London but also that they had just bought, for cash, a new office in the hallowed ground of No 1 Lothbury.

That all said, the problems for the businessman or woman embarking on business remain pretty well unchanged – just how does one deal with a Chinese supplier going silent after positive discussions in China and splendid celebratory meals? How can we, firstly, understand the actions of the PRC Government and from a business perspective, read the motivations and aspirations of the people with whom we trade, their attitudes to money and to ownership?

I hope the new edition sheds light on this fascinating nation and am delighted that my friend Yingshi Helsby has agreed to add her own Chinese culture and language perspective to unlocking this riddle at a time of enormous potential change for China as the relatively youthful. Xi Jinping 习近平 (Xí Jìnpíng) (born 15 June 1953) has been anointed as the new Head of the Communist Party of China during the recent 18th National Congress. He was also significantly given immediate command of China's military as Chairman of the Communist Party of China Central Committee and Vice Chairman of the PRX Central Military Commission. These positions were hitherto retained by outgoing leaders until the new man had served his apprenticeship. He became China's head of state, the President, at the fourth plenary meeting of the first session of the 12th National People's Congress (NPC) in Beijing on 14th March 2013. He was also elected Chairman of the Central Military Commission of the PRC and was, crucially, appointed General Secretary of the Communist Party of China. Xi takes over after Hu Jintao 胡锦涛 (Hú Jǐntāo)'s ten years of cautious rule and observers look to a period of change from this, only the second peaceful, transfer of power in China's history.

2

CHINA AND ITS HISTORY
IN BRIEF

The People's Republic of China 中华人民共和国 (Zhōnghuá Rénmín Gònghéguó), commonly known as China, is the third largest country in the world and occupies one-fifteenth of the world's landmass. There are twenty three provinces including Taiwan; five autonomous regions: Inner Mongolia 内蒙古 (Nèiménggǔ), Guangxi 广西 (Guǎngxi), Tibet 西藏 (Xīzàng), Ningxia 宁夏 (Níngxià), Xinjiang 新疆 (Xīnjiāng); four provincial-level municipalities, Beijing (Peking) 北京 (Běijīng), Tianjin 天津 (Tiānjīn), Shanghai 上海 (Shànghǎi) and Chongqing (Chungking) 重庆 (Chóngqìng); two Special Administrative Regions: Hong Kong 香港 (Xiānggǎng), and Macao 澳门 (Àomén). China regained the long-held colonies of Hong Kong from Britain in 1997 and Macau from Portugal in 1999. The capital is Beijing.

Map of China 中国地图 (Zhōngguó dìtú)

Administrative Divisions of the
People's Republic of China (PRC)

China has two of the world's greatest rivers. The Yellow River 黄河 (Huánghé) is 5,464 kilometres long and the longer Yangtze 长江 (Chángjiāng) (6,300 kilometres) cut across China to provide vital transport links. In the North-West, China is a sparsely settled region of high mountains, steppes and deserts. The South-West contains the plateau of Tibet, which meets the Himalayas. In the centre there are river basins and in the east plains, deltas, and hills. Jungles and tropical lowlands lie in southeast. The Eastern coast region is lined with prosperous cities and ports. The climate ranges from the bitter winters of frigid Northern China to the hot and humid monsoon seasons of the south and is varied and extreme. The standard time used throughout China is eight hours ahead of the Universal Time Coordinated (UTC+8).

China is the most populated nation on earth, making up roughly one-fifth of the world's population. The official language in China is Mandarin Chinese, which is one of the six working languages at the United Nations. China officially recognizes 56 distinct ethnic groups today, the largest of which is the dominant Han Chinese, who constitute about 92% of the total population. Most of the 56 minority nationalities have their own languages and endeavour to maintain their equally distinctive dress and culture in the face of rapid development. China's geography causes an uneven population distribution with 94% living in the eastern third of the country and the remainder amongst western deserts, high plateaux and mountains.

Officially atheist, China is a however a multi-religious country embracing Buddhism, Taoism and Islam as the three major religions. Catholicism and Protestantism have smaller but substantial followings today especially in the increasingly prosperous middle-class. Ancestor worship is a theme that transcends all the traditional Chinese religions. Confucianism is a philosophy which most Chinese people follow and behind all this lie millennia of folk-belief surrounding good and bad fortune, numbers, symbols and colours.

To bring matters back to the current business world it is worth taking a look at the basic statistical differences between China, UK and the USA:

China	UK	USA
1.4 billion people	61 million people	0.3 billion people (313 million people)
92% Han Chinese (the largest ethnic group in the world.)	92% White	80% White
56 recognized minority groups	8 main minority groups	6 main minority groups
9.6 million square km	0.24 million square km	9.8 million square km

The Communist Party of China (CPC) has governed China since the state's establishment in 1949. This sole political organization is divided into Executive, Legislative and Judicial branches with a voice for the Minority Races at the centre of Government which seems only reasonable since all Chinese passports state the bearer's race.

The President is head of state and the Premier is head of government and they are elected for five-year terms at the National People's Congress. China provides nine-year compulsory education for its young although the nation will continue to face a shortage of places in tertiary education beyond 2015 in spite of its One Child Policy.

Information from China's Sixth Census 2010 第六次人口普查 (2010 dìliùcì rénkǒu pǔchá) reveals more about the current standards of living:

- Population growth rate: 0.655%,
- GDP (purchasing power parity): $8.767 trillion,
- GDP per Capita: U.S. $4,700
- GDP – real growth rate: 8.4%,
- Labour force: 812.7 million,
- Industrial production growth rate: 8.1%,
- Unemployment rate: 4.3%
- Life Expectancy: 71
- Literacy Percentage: 94%

A brief history of China

To put China's extremely long recorded history in some kind of digestible context we can split the millennia into various distinct periods and major dynasties:

Xia Dynasty 夏朝 (Xiàcháo)	before 1650 b.c.	Dating estimates from archeological sites
Shang Dynasty 商朝 (Shāngcháo)	1650-1027 b.c.	Mencius and Confucius teaching on moral values started
Qin Dynasty 秦朝 (Qíncháo)	221 b.c.	Qin Shihuang 秦始皇 (Qínshǐhuáng) was the first emperor unified China, established central government, standardised the written language. His tomb is in Xi'an, well known for its terra cotta guards and horses. The Great Wall was largely complete.

Han Dynasty 汉朝 (Hàncháo)	206 b.c. to 220 a.d.	China became a powerful empire, a golden age in art, politics, and technology. Started trading with the Middle East by way of the Silk Road through Central Asia, reaching the Roman Empire. The first Chinese encyclopedia was compiled. Paper was invented. Buddhism was introduced from India. Started enduring bureaucracy based on intellect rather than aristocratic birth. Ethnic Chinese are still referred to as 'Han' today.
Sui Dynasty 隋朝 (Suícháo)	581-618	Unification of China after long period of divided rule and civil war – Three Kingdoms. Extensive canals were built, interconnecting the Yellow River – Huanghe 黄河 (Huánghé) and the Yangtze River – Changjiang 长江 (Chángjiāng). Chinese political structure, art, and literature were exported to Korea during this time.
Tang Dynasty 唐朝 (Tángcháo)	618-907	A long period of prosperity and great cultural accomplishment in music, literature (including poetry), painting, sculpture, and architecture. Porcelain, invented during the Han Dynasty, came into mass production. Buddhist monasteries were curtailed, and Islam took root and spread. Tea drinking became widespread. Chinese culture starts influencing Japan via Korea.
Song Dynasty 宋朝 (Sòngcháo)	960-1263	More prosperity and great cultural accomplishment. The empire made Neo-Confucianism the official state philosophy. The compass, movable typeset and gun-powder for military purposes were developed. Population was over 100 million for the first time.
Yuan Dynasty 元朝 (Yuáncháo)	1279-1365	The Mongols conquered and controlled China under Kublai Khan and moved the capital to Beijing. Grand Canal connecting north and south China was completed. In literature, drama was in its most vigorous period. The Dalai Lama was established with Tibet becoming a vassal state of China.
Ming Dynasty 明朝 (Míngcháo)	1368-1644	Emperor Zhudi's eunuch admiral Zhenghe explored the world. Portuguese arrived by ship in 1514, regular trade with Europe was begun. The Ming rebuilt and added to the Great Wall. In the early 1400s, Ming dominated Asian waters as far as Arabia.

Qing Dynasty 清朝 (Qīngcháo)	1644-1911	The Manchus greatly extended the power of the Chinese Empire to Outer Mongolia, Tibet, Taiwan, and Chinese Turkestan.
		A classic novel, *The Dream of the Red Chamber*, published.
		From the 1830s to the early 1860s, China was beset by several revolts. The most serious was the Taiping Rebellion in 1850.
		In the 1880s, China lost two of its tributary states: Annam to France and Burma to Great Britain. After the Sino-Japanese War (1894-95), China ceded Taiwan and the Pescadores to Japan and renounced claims to Korea.
		In the late 1890s the Western powers received additional concessions and territory.
		China was forced to accept a proposal put forth by the United States in 1899 that all nations be granted equal commercial opportunity in China.
		Chinese imperialism ended.
	1839-42	China lost the Opium War to Great Britain.
		In 1842, the Treaty of Nanjing gave Hong Kong to the United Kingdom and allowed the British to trade at five Chinese ports.
China proclaimed a republic	1911-1949	A republic experiments with parliamentary government led by Sun Yat-sen, later Yuan Shihkai, but Yuan turned to dictatorship. General Chiang Kai-shek 蒋介石 (Jiǎngjièshí) became head of the Kuomintang government in 1926.
		Outer Mongolia declared itself independent in 1911. Tibet followed in 1913, but China later reclaimed it.
		Traditional customs, such as the wearing of the queue (pigtail) by men and the binding of women's feet, were being abandoned.
	1934-1935	Mao Zedong led between 100,000 and 190,000 Chinese Communists on their 10,000 kilometre Long March from south-west China to Shaanxi in the north – 20,000 survived.
	1931-1945	The Japanese invaded China.

People's Republic of China	1949	The Chinese Communists defeated the Nationalists and established the People's Republic of China. China started rebuilding transportation networks and industry. Private ownership of business was virtually eliminated. Large-scale land reform was carried out.
	1958	The Communists launched the Great Leap Forward, which severely weakened China's economy.
	1966-1969	The Cultural Revolution disrupted education, the government, and daily life in China.
	1971	China was admitted to the United Nations.
	1972	US President Richard M. Nixon visited China.
	1976	Communist Party Chairman Mao Zedong 毛泽东 Máozédōng and Premier Zhou Enlai 周恩来 (Zhōu'ēnlái) died. Deng Xiaoping 邓小平 (Dèngxiǎopíng) started leading China, began reforms toward reducing government economic controls and transformed the economy.
	1979	China and the United States established normal diplomatic relations.
	1989	Demonstrations across China called for more democracy and an end to corruption in government.
	1997	Deng Xiaoping died. Deng was succeeded by Jiang Zemin 江泽民 (Jiāngzémín). China regained control of Hong Kong from the United Kingdom. Hong Kong became a Special Administrative Region of China, and applying the 'one country, two systems', its capitalist system will remain in effect for 50 years.
	1999	China regained control of Macao from Portugal and impose law and order on the gambling enclave.

China is one of the world's oldest continuous civilizations and the longest of the four ancient civilizations. She has a written history of more than 4,000 years alternating between periods of political unity and disunity and in that time has been occasionally conquered by external groups of people, some of whom were eventually assimilated into the Chinese population.

There has been human habitation in China since prehistoric times – 1,700,000 years ago when Yuanmou Man 元谋人 (Yuánmóu Rén), the earliest man was found in China in Yunnan Province.

Chinese history is normally described in relation to Dynasties. The common characteristic of Chinese rule is that there was one primary leader – the Emperor of China. Each emperor was succeeded by another, usually by birthright, until an opposing group took power. At times, two or more Dynasties coexisted in different parts of China. A Chinese Dynasty often began with a very powerful leader, developed over a period of time to a highly successful civilization, then degraded, after some upheaval, eventually taken over by a new one.

Major Chinese dynasties and modern history

The first historical emperor of China was the Yellow Emperor 黄帝 (Huángdì) who is considered to be the ancestor of all Han Chinese and the visionary who established the nation of China. So successful was he that he spent much of his and his scholars' efforts in his latter years in attempting to guarantee his immortality.

We have detailed records dating from this time on agriculture and silk-making from both the Xia 夏 (Xià) and Shang 商 (Shāng) Dynasties. During the Zhou 周 (Zhōu) dynasty, China was the most advanced bronze-working civilization in the world.

The Taoist philosopher Zhuangzi 庄子 (Zhuāngzi) (350-275 b.c.) first proclaimed the principles of the 'Mandate of Heaven' by which Emperors ruled the nation through the good will of his subjects . Confucius lived after the Song Dynasty, a time called Chun Qiu 春秋 (Chūnqiū), a transnational period before the Qin 秦 (Qín) dynasty. The famous book *The Art of War* by Sunzi 孙子 (Sūnzi) was also written at this time and this book has been embraced by Western business schools for its lessons in tactics and out-thinking opponents.

The Qin Emperor 秦始皇 (Qín Shǐhuáng) unified China and ruled a vast territory. He standardised Chinese characters, weights and measures. He started building the Great Wall of China to fend off nomadic invasion from the north. He also relied heavily on strict legal codes and to silence criticism of his imperial rule, he banished or put to death many dissenting Confucian scholars, confiscating and burning their books. It is interesting to note that Chairman Mao similarly simplified a common Chinese written form and imposed a unified Chinese spoken form – Putonghua – the Standard Speech.

Dissenting scholars once more suffered grievously during the Great Proletarian Cultural Revolution with many being banished to a far-off place called Luzhou 庐州 (Lú zhōu) near Hefei city in Anhui Province in Eastern China where the intellectuals later invented the CD.

The later emperor Liubang 刘邦 (Liúbāng) founded the Han Dynasty applying much less harsh rule and encouraging and overseeing stunning technological advances such as paper and porcelain.

The Han Dynasty was followed by the Jin 金 (Jīn) Dynasty which was founded by the Wanyan 完顏 (Wányán) clan of the Jurchens, the ancestors of the Manchus from the north. After many years of civil war, the Sui Dynasty was born. It reunified Southern and Northern China and reduced the social gap between the rich and the poor.

Historians regard the Tang Dynasty as the high point in Chinese civilization. The Tang period was the golden age of literature and art in China. Tang rule also perfected a government system supported by a large class of Confucian literati selected through civil service examinations.

In 960 a.d., the Song Dynasty came to power. This was the first government in world history to issue paper money. This dynasty also saw the first known use of gunpowder as well as first discernment of true north using a compass.

It was during the Yuan Dynasty that Marco Polo arrived from Italy in about 1268 and wrote about the splendour of the Mongol Empire from the then capital Karakorum. He wrote of his extensive travels throughout Asia on behalf of the Khan, and their eventual return after 15,000 miles and 24 years of adventures.

The Chinese Fleet of the Ming dynasty sailed the China seas and the Indian Ocean, reaching as far as the east coast of Africa. Toward the end of the dynasty, long wars with the Mongols and incursions by the Japanese into Korea weakened Ming rule, which resulted in foreign takeovers.

In 1644 the Manchu tribe took Beijing and establishing the last imperial dynasty – the Qing. Qing rulers nonetheless put into effect measures aimed at preventing the absorption of the Manchu into the dominant Han Chinese population. Han Chinese were prohibited from migrating into the Manchu homeland and Manchu were forbidden to engage in trade or manual labour. Intermarriage between the two groups was forbidden.

The Kangxi Dictionary 康熙字典 (Kāngxī zìdiǎn) the first standard Chinese dictionary was published during this Dynasty in 1716 and set down many radicals (the constituent parts of written Chinese characters) still in use today.

The highly influential and culturally rich Song, Yuan, Ming, and Qing Dynasties all lasted for about 300 years and all played a major role in the long historical journey of the Chinese people as they created a culture with strong philosophies, traditions and values.

The Five Elements in Chinese thought and culture

The Chinese believe that we are surrounded by the Five Elements 五行 (Wǔháng) of Chinese astrology – the Earth Element 土 (tǔ), the Fire Element 火 (huǒ), the Water Element 水 (shuǐ), the Metal Element 金 (jīn) and the Wood Element 木 (mù). Everything can be described in terms of the Five Elements. Each represents a phase in a cycle of being and all constantly interact, moving and changing as life goes on. Harmony lies in balancing the five elements as each element acts upon two others, either giving birth to it or controlling it.

The Five Elements still affect Chinese thought deeply, just like Newton's Law of Gravity affects us in the west.

In traditional Chinese medicine, the Five Elements correspond to different parts of the body. A person becomes ill because the balance in their body is lost and so to heal a sick person one must balance them. The elements as they correspond to the body:

- Wood: liver, gall bladder, eyes, tendons, tears, sight
- Fire: heart, small intestine, tongue, pulse, sweat, speech
- Earth: spleen/pancreas, stomach, mouth, muscles, saliva, taste
- Metal: lungs, large intestine, nose, skin, mucus, smell
- Water: kidneys, bladder, ears, bones, urine, hearing

Another example, Chinese Cuisine, is similarly based on the five elements. A good Chinese meal should not only be delicious to taste but also have the five elements in balance. The elements represented in foods are:

- Wood: sour
- Fire: bitter
- Earth: sweet
- Metal: pungent (sometimes termed as spicy)
- Water: salty

The Five Elements are also reflected in many aspects of Chinese life, including agriculture, martial arts, traditional works of Chinese astronomy, music, feng shui, and fortune-telling, as well as in people's relationships.

3

DECODING THE NEW CHINESE CONUNDRUM

Behaviour patterns in context

There is a mass of learned data on the cultural obstacles facing business men and women working across radically different cultures and much in the way of 'How to do business in China' but relatively little on the behaviour patterns and cultural issues involved. That is what this book sets out to provide. Cultural differences have led to an atmosphere in which little is expected to happen quickly when western business set up in China but without really understanding why. By working through this book you will quickly pick up a wide range of skills in handling the local situation. In this enlarged edition we have endeavoured to explain the background to the Chinese cultural mind-set in detail and in readily accessible terms. At the back of the book you will find some tables for guidance if you find yourself in an awkward situation, along with business and inter-cultural notes for your quick reference when you are out and about.

Some inter-cultural concepts

To understand your Chinese business counterpart you do not need to be an academic or a linguist but by borrowing a few of the key inter-cultural concepts plus their insights, you can save a lot of your time, money and personal frustration.

The Business Culture – Garrison's Iceberg Model

An immensely influential British thinker, Professor Terry Garrison of Henley Management College, deserves close attention. The Iceberg and the Triangle Test are two of his creations that give immediate insights for the business reader.

The Iceberg looks into how cultures of all kinds are formed. If we think of a national culture, that part we see with our own eyes, as the tip of an iceberg, and then drill down to what has produced this then we can quickly pick out the key drivers. What we see on a daily basis at the tip of this vast chunk of frozen cultural water is the structure and the function of society – its sociology, the mental characteristics and attitudes of people and groups – their psychology and finally, societies' organization, evolution and customs – its anthropology. What actually goes to produce this complex picture is the influence of another and deeper group of features – history, geography, economics, politics and religion/ideology.

So, let's look how business cultures are formed. If we think of a national culture, that part we see with our own eyes, as the tip of an iceberg, and then drill down to what has produced this then we can quickly pick out the key drivers. What we see on a daily basis is the structure and the function of society, its sociology, the mental characteristics and attitudes of people and groups, their psychology and finally, societies' evolution and customs, its anthropology.

What actually goes to produce this complex picture is partly the influence of a nation's history which influences people in the present. To this day Scots, for example, find it very hard to forget their defeat at the hands of the English (and anti-Jacobite Scots) in 1746 and fourth generation Australians feel enormous pride at being able to trace their family history back to luckless felons transported to Botany Bay for some crime, great or trivial.

A nation's geography, be it desert or lush farmland, landlocked or coastal, has a deep influence on how groups of people live and think. Think how many languages the Danes have found it necessary to learn with so many powerful neighbours surrounding them and how linguistically isolationist the British have been able to be as a robust island nation whose influence has led much of the globe to speak English. Or, right at the present time, we need only glance at the industrious German nation who had perforce to move their agrarian economy on the inhospitable north European Plain to be the industrial powerhouse of Europe after being crushed in two World Wars. Not only that, they then ploughed through a reunification of West and East which many thought or hoped might at worst impoverish German once more or at best keep them too busy sorting out a tapestry of political, economic and social conundra to readjust to became a threat again and then, lo, they become the lead nation in Europe with the willingness, political leverage and economic resource to lift the drowning Euro, a.k.a. Europe, out of its cataclysmic borrowing and accounting horror.

Next, the economics of a nation will make people think, feel and act in different ways – for example the effect of the soup queues and desperate drive west in the USA as the land was exhausted during the Depression and could no longer produce crops. At the other extreme, the tension between the vast oil wealth of Saudi Arabia's ruling families who hold on to their deeply traditional way of life and the relative poverty of the of the commoners feeling increasingly disenfranchised yet empowered in the wake of the Arab Spring.

The politics of a nation, whilst a product of national circumstances, in its own turn produces different mindsets in its people. Graphic examples of this would be the determined pursuit and achievement of great wealth and status in Hong Kong by penniless refugees during the latter part of the 20th Century when colonial government was exercised by 'positive non-interventionism' in contrast to the grinding poverty and political oppression across the Shumchun River in Mainland China in the days of a doomed communist command economy. Chairman Mao was struggling to hold on to power at whatever cost but in Hong Kong the commercial majority sought peace and quiet as assured by the Colonial administration under which to amass money. Across the Shumchun River it was a matter of either expedient, or genuine, and vocal support for a Communist Party which had reunified the nation but under which never was it truer that it was the upright nail that always got hammered flat.

Closely related to politics is religion/ideology, which plays a great part too in producing the veneer of society. In America many believe that they have an inalienable right to bear arms and see themselves as upholding traditions vital to the future of their nation and their creed in no way related to the gun-carrying criminal fraternity.

Put all these five driving influences of geography, economy, politics, religion and ideology into the swirling waters which produces this cultural iceberg and one begins to understand a great deal more about why people are the way they are.

The Chinese Cultural Iceberg

We constantly see how people interact, how they think and how they behave and can now comprehend why much of this is. However, it is what produces the different way the Chinese act that interest us here. China's immense and varied landscape, the huge energy created everywhere by her recent economic success, the tensions in her capitalist socialist government, belief systems revolving around Daoism, then Confucianism, Buddhism, Communism with lately, Capitalism intermingled with her recorded and revered history all go together to produce an impressive list of boom cities such as Hong Kong, Shanghai, Beijing, Shenzhen, Macau, Guangzhou, Tianjin, Dongguan, Foshan and Dalian. These form the ten most competitive cities according to the National Bureau of Statistics 2009-2010 report (Xu Z L and Nong Z) but interestingly omits mention of the long-growing central-Chinese powerhouse of Chongqing.

China used to be a society based on family and the work unit but now revolves increasingly around work to the detriment of the former. The nation is awash with business opportunities of all kinds and despite its highly structured systems of behaviour offers tantalising promise of unimaginable wealth. All in an erstwhile Communist State where only a generation ago one's university and career were all decided by the State and following the Capitalist Road was enough to have one thrown to mobs of Party zealots. The aforementioned boom cities have developed from raw sites in which the People's Armed Police have had to struggle to maintain law and order into prosperous and safe international business centres full of pride at their very Chinese model of success. Why then, do the Chinese behave the way they do?

So let us look a little more deeply into China's Iceberg and see what we can discern by beginning from the base of the iceberg grinding away under the surface of the imaginary surface of the sea and about to be filtered through theory and then move to the visible tip of the Iceberg, let us look again at her history. We have seen its having been recorded over 4 millennia which is one reason why that and her ancient language are sources of such deep great pride to its people. The foreigner who acknowledges this will have moved a long way to building solid business relations or *guanxi*.

The very immensity of her recently reunited landmass makes China's geography a particularly powerful influence on her people. For instance, her area of 3.7 million square miles/9.6 million square kilometres necessarily means borders with other countries. The 14 thousand miles / 22 thousand kilometres China shares with neighbours large and small, powerful and weak and friendly and aggressive has given her a reputation for both consolidating her territory or blatantly expanding it dependant upon which nation's standpoint one takes. Her relationship with the USSR varies from close to hostile whilst those with India and Vietnam have remained sensitive.

It is not hard to see why she is sensitive about geographical security let alone foreign expansion. Add to this a 9,010 mile-long / 14,500 kilometres coastline and one can easily see why China feels the need to defend her land, airspace and seas. Turn the coin the other way and huge opportunities for international trade and political influence appear for these very reasons.

Everyone is aware of China's economic success. Even accepting that some massaging of output and profit has probably been in play, her achievements have been immense and have propelled her into international prominence and power. China has such a vast appetite for raw materials that the global prices of fuel, cement, steel and copper have rocketed, affecting consumers in all countries. Not content with existing sources of supply, China has built on her position as Champion of the Third World to extend her involvement across Africa, building roads and railways which in turn ease access to Africa's resources. Large numbers of Chinese have moved into Africa and the Middle East increasing the already vast Chinese diaspora, but this time with the overt blessing of Central Government.

Politics in China have long intrigued external observers. A

romantic view of the secretive and wealthy Celestial Kingdom ruled by Emperors and Empresses guided by powerful cliques of eunuchs moved through deep indignation at the disdain and sometimes extreme violence with which Western envoys were treated as Britain, Germany and the USA tried to carve up China for themselves. This in turn led to mixed reactions after the collapse of the ruling dynasty and China writhed in decades of impoverishing civil war. The victor, Chairman Mao Zedong, first courted the USSR for aid in building the newly re-unified China and this communism bred deep mistrust in the West as they dealt with their own worries over the Russian Bear during the Cold War. It was only relatively recently that US President Richard Nixon led the way for the western nations to open dialogues with China and re-establish trading links.

Throughout the 20th Century though, the fear of communism tainted all dealings and this still exists. The power of the Chinese Communist Party is absolute and Maoist philosophy has inspired guerrillas from Malaya to colonial Hong Kong and once monarchist Nepal. The recent popular revival of Mao and his policies was further fuelled by the disgraced high-flying politician Bo Xilai; he struck a real chord with the populace as worries over inflation led many to look back in fondness to the order of Mao's totalitarian rule whereas others remembered only too well the mayhem and horrors of the Great Cultural Proletarian Revolution, Tiananmen Square and other aberrations created to maintain power and social stability.

China's ideology is rich in Maoist thinking and that is no surprise given the effort that he took in rebuilding his country. Whatever disasters he occasioned or survived, there are few in China who do not admire his achievement in reunifying China. The emotional and cultural sense of being 'Chinese' is something that must be acknowledged in any dealings with her people. Unlike the comparatively recently reunified Italy where it is more important whether one comes from the North or the South than to come from 'Italy', Chinese people be they from UK, USA, Taiwan, the PRC or the Oman, see themselves as Chinese first and foremost. In this respect they are not unlike the Scots – think for example of Highland Games and Clan Gatherings in Nova Scotia where the descendants of immigrants driven abroad by their clan chieftains during the Highland Clearances of the 18th

and 19th Centuries celebrate their ethnicity or the Commanding Officer of a US aircraft carrier whose early morning joy was to play his bagpipes on the upper deck of his command as was his right as an ethnic Scot. Understanding this sense of ethnic identity is crucial to understanding the Chinese – it is a source of enormous personal pride and a sensitivity to be trifled with considerable care. As central to being Chinese is the influence of Confucius and that is dealt with separately in this tome.

Over this we must lay a huge enthusiasm for Capitalism. This has become an enormous driver of Chinese society and its effects have been immense, yet not always positive when one sees increasing need of social welfare provision.

We can now see the nation, not as a harmonious whole, but rather, as a number of deeply dysfunctional elements generally intent on profitable modernisation with elements in profound disagreement whether for ethical, religious or behavioural reasons.

The diagram overleaf provides a graphic illustration of the Chinese cultural iceberg, based on Terry Garrison's model:

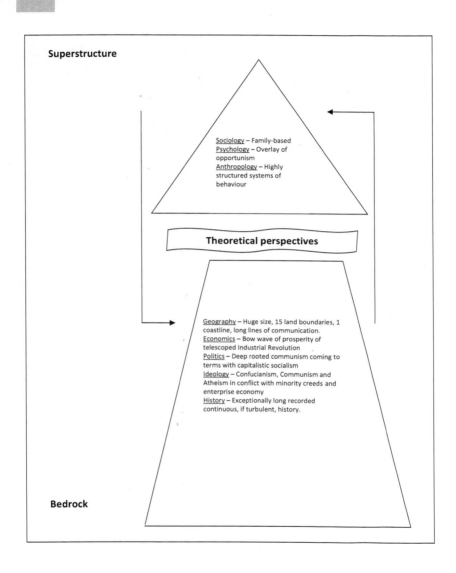

China's Iceberg Model
(adapted from Terry Garrison)

In laying out the theory behind the Iceberg Model, Garrison defines culture as

> *all about organisational identity and relational predictability... it deals with the social rules of group existence and conduct.*

and so he divides his Iceberg into two segments. In China you will see a super-structure of the visible, tangible aspects of group culture and below that the less easily perceived bedrock elements from which the former is thrown up. These are of huge relevance and their inter-relationships allow us to see the many conflicts at work deep below the relatively calm surface of this apparently unstoppable economic giant.

Secondly, he devised a National Business Culture Test, which examines nations by Entrepreneurship, Systems Rigidity, Leadership and Social Protection. This can give us in the business community further insight into our Chinese partners. Our research reveals an economy seized wholeheartedly by the opportunities to make money on an unprecedented scale but still under the firm control of a one-party state nervous at the effects of this individual growth in wealth in only certain areas.

National Business Culture Test – PRC	
Entrepreneurship	**Systems rigidity**
High growth orientation. Government and individuals have sustained growth well in excess of current 8% in face of global economic downturn. Her performance now eclipses that of Japan. Strategy of economic modernization continues as state-owned enterprises are denationalized. Some uncertainty and unemployment may destabilise nation.	High systems rigidity. Government maintains systems over political, religious, bureaucratic and, still, social facets. Communist party demands Groupthink from its leaders in guise of paternalism. State Planning Committee and its subordinate departments wield great control with some considerable support of the people as means to keep development under bureaucratic control and maintaining administrative systems. On going acceptance of dilution of national policy at local level
Highly entrepreneurial – Government stimulating economy correctly plus personal scramble to 'catch the chance'.	
Recidivism still marked in its control mechanisms in place over all forms of foreign investment but this coexists with national trading orientation.	

Leadership	Social protection
Highly authoritative. Post-Deng Xiaoping, the PRC has maintained a growth of GDP, which belies an absence of old-style political leadership. Doctrinal purity still pursued in terms of stamping out 'troublemaking' sects – Muslims, Falun Gong – corruption and keeping check on pace of economic development; leadership by the State. Some space for consensus in commercial areas.	Balance of exploitation and support. UK's Department for International Development is stepping in to assist with setting up Unemployment Insurance and Employment Services (UIES) as the Chinese State has accepted the need to balance high growth with social responsibility. Distribution of income liable to create unrest as the less advantaged see opportunity gap widen. Necessity to grow without alienating majority of population. It is estimated that 90% of Chinese make no contribution to growth by virtue of their lack of opportunity. This explains state's continued heavy-handedness against the corrupt and wealthy.

Conclusion
China has now wholeheartedly seized the issue of economic change and development as essential for its future. It still seeks to maintain its Party systems whilst seeking the advantages of capitalism – in taking back Hong Kong it sought one nation and two systems. Culture shock is on going.

Analysis of Chinese Business Culture using Garrison's Model

Triangle Test

The last of Terry Garrison's models we will look at is his Triangle Test that plots groups by Bedrock Culture as above, Work Systems Posture and Behaviour Patterns. This enables decisions on multi-cultural management issues, mergers and strategic moves to be made with reasoned confidence. The Triangle Test needs samples of at least 20 people from each group under inspection to give a useable spread and a reasonably correct picture of responses on the individuals' own behaviours, the nature of their work systems and the political, economic & religious drivers in their countries. In this case use was made of indicative primary and secondary date in each country with executives on UK MBA courses and also working in China.

It is recognised that in some nations, merely asking a cultural question could produce an overtly emotional response since the very fact of asking could be seen as value laden in itself. The reason for this is that culture has more to do with personal values and feelings rather than personality. Both sides in a relationship need to know the key areas in which the deepest held values exist and the Triangle Tool helps re-examine these in visual terms.

Test responses were answered on a scale from '1' – "I disagree entirely with this proposition or statement" through to '5' – "I agree totally with this proposition or statement", using questions adapted from Garrison and designed to be as neutral possible in social science terms but recognising that given the conversational format there might always be some possible bias.

Use was not made of '0' to indicate a 'non' response in this instance since deductive use was made of the some secondary data used.

Firstly, let us look at what was revealed about China:

A.   *Bedrock Culture*

		Question	Answer
		Do you agree that in China….	Individualist 1 >Corporatist 5
1		Chinese shareholders are anxious to keep Chinese companies in national hands and not allow them to be acquired by foreigners?	4
2		Chinese shareholders are less interested in the value of their shares than the nationality of the shareholders?	4
3		The system in China allows the ownership of Chinese companies to be protected in such a way that they cannot be acquired by foreign companies?	1
4		Chinese companies have relationships with any other institutions (government, bank, etc) which allow them to obtain debt capital at preferential rates?	4
5		Chinese companies are driven by longer-term strategic considerations than by short-term financial considerations (such as the level of the share price, dividends, etc)?	4
6		Chinese companies run more to meet the requirements of all its stakeholders – shareholders, workers and management – than to satisfy its shareholders?	4
7		If Chinese companies should fail financially, they would expect help from other national institution (such as a bank) because of the relationship it has with that institution?	3
8		The Chinese government and/or the civil service are involved in helping to advise on, plan or co-ordinate key aspects of companies' commercial activities, with companies' agreement?	3

9	The workforce are systematically consulted upon matters of strategic importance (e.g. product innovation, wage policy, redundancy) by Chinese companies?	<u>2</u>
10	The financial rewards of managers and workers in Chinese companies (wages, salaries, bonuses, etc) are related more to tradition or national pay settlements than to their specific on-the-job performance?	3

Average = 3.2

China is shown as still retaining reducing classic Corporatist values as culture shifts towards individualism.

B. *Culture Posture*

	Question **Do you agree that in China….**	**Answer** Communitarian 1 >Materialistic 5
11	The economy of China is developing quickly and strongly? Is there a mood of growth-related optimism and evidence of innovation in the business community? Are there more signs here of dynamic entrepreneurship than there of static resistance to change?	<u>5</u>
12	The government and/or the country's major businesses are forcing through change in an authoritarian manner without much consideration of the interests of those affected by change? Such consideration might typically involve substantive and consensual discussion with lobby group and interested parties such as the trade union movement. Is such discussion taking place?	<u>3</u>
13	The current development of China's economy is matched by a willing acceptance of innovatory changes in working practices (pay, hiring, redundancy, training, worker representation in decision-making, etc) rather than a bureaucratic resistance by the workforce in most companies?	<u>3</u>
14	The business community feeling in China is generally that social protection systems (e.g. welfare state, unemployment benefit systems) are increasingly outdated and unaffordable? Is there an exploitative mood among business leaders that states that 'changes is necessary whatever the social cost' rather than a feeling that workers must be protected against changes which are too fast and too large? How strong is this mood?	2

Average = 3.25

In the rush to get wealthy culture is moving towards an increasingly materialistic posture.

C. *Behaviour patterns*

		Question	Answer
		Do you agree that in China….	Closed 1 >Open 5
15		Business people in China tend to speak plainly about what they want? Do they tend to want to be specific, even if sometimes undiplomatic, because they want to avoid any misunderstanding? Are they uncomfortable with silences and atmospheres they cannot understand? [Authors' Note – this will also depend on what stage of guanxi discussions are taking place]	3
16		Business people in China are naturally friendly towards their foreign counterparts? Do they tend to develop real friendships even in business relatively quickly? Are they **not** very much concerned with embarrassment or loss of face?	4
17		The business community in China is relatively informal about how people deal with one another? For example, to what extent does the business fraternity avoid laying down rules and codes of behaviour about how you dress (in business situations) or speak (to superiors or subordinates) or act (bowing with deference and respect, for example to a superior)? Is impoliteness sometimes seen as acceptable?	2
18		Business people in China seem to have a natural tendency towards impatience and decisiveness? Do they always want to get on with things? Do they tend to be restive with a lot of debate about what to do? Do they usually want quick results, reckoning that actions speak louder than words?	2

Average = 2.40

The business sample scored close to mid-way between being an open and being a closed community when it came to the way they saw behaviour and this indicates a substantial move away from deep-rooted Communism.

It can now be seen how China tends towards the classic Asian model of high Corporatism (Sector A, 3.2) and Materialism (Sector B, 3.25) although nowadays it displays neither Closed nor Open behaviour values (Sector C, 2.4) as its society changes under increasing contact with the West, no longer a classic Asian 'Triple C' society in Garrison's terminology.

When a similar sample of British executives were polled the following picture began to emerge.

UK General Population

A.   Bedrock Culture

	Question	Answer
		Individualist 1 >Corporatist 5
1	Are UK nationals anxious to keep UK business in national hands and not allow it to be acquired by foreigners?	3
2	Are UK nationals less interested in the value of their business than the nationality of the owner?	2
3	Does the system in UK allow the ownership of local concerns to be protected in such a way that they cannot be acquired by foreigners?	1
4	Do UK businesses have relationships with any other institutions (government, bank, etc) which allow them to obtain debt capital at preferential rates?	2
5	To what extent are UK nationals driven by longer term strategic considerations than by short-term financial considerations?	2
6	Are UK towns, cities and villages run more to meet the requirements of all locals – than to satisfy its councils?	3
7	If UK companies should fail financially, to what extent would they expect help from any other national institution (such as a bank) because of the relationship it has with that institution?	1
8	To what extent are the UK government and/or the civil service involved in helping to advise on, plan or co-ordinate key aspects of commercial activities, with locals' agreement?	3
9	To what extent is the workforce systematically consulted upon matters of strategic importance (e.g. product innovation, wage policy, redundancy) by their managers?	3
10	To what extent are the financial rewards of leaders and electorate in UK (salaries, bonuses, etc) related more to tradition or national pay settlements than to their specific on-the-job performance?	3

Average = 2.3

A slight tendency towards the Individualist end of this spectrum in response to feelings of lack of governmental support and economic worries.

B.   Culture Posture

	Question	Answer
		Communitarian 1 >Materialistic 5
11	To what extent is the economy of UK developing quickly and strongly? Is there a mood of growth-related optimism and evidence of innovation in the business community? Are there more signs here of dynamic entrepreneurship than there of static resistance to change?	1
12	To what extent are the government and/or UK's local businesses forcing through change in an authoritarian manner without much consideration of the interests of those affected by change? Such consideration might typically involve substantive and consensual discussion with lobby group and interested parties such as the trade union movement. Is such discussion taking place?	2
13	To what extent is the current development of UK's economy matched by a willing acceptance of innovatory changes in working practices (pay, hiring, redundancy, training, worker representation in decision-making, etc) rather than a bureaucratic resistance by the workforce in most companies?	4
14	How strong is the community feeling in UK generally that social protection systems (e.g. welfare state, unemployment benefit systems) are increasingly outdated and unaffordable? Is there an exploitative mood among business leaders that states that 'changes is necessary whatever the social cost' rather than a feeling that workers must be protected against changes which are too fast and too large? How strong is this mood?	4

Average = 3.75

The Thatcher years now being a long way the past and society increasingly divided between the very wealthy and the remainder, there has been a slight move away from total materialism and a shift towards more traditional quasi-family values. The UK family unit has changed enormously but indications are that the less formal partnering bonds now being established across and within the sexes are as permanent and as mutually sustaining as the church wedding.

C. *Behaviour patterns*

	Question	Answer
		Closed 1 >Open 5
15	To what extent do UK nationals tend to speak plainly about what they want? Do they tend to want to be specific, even if sometimes undiplomatic, because they want to avoid any misunderstanding? Are they uncomfortable with silences and atmospheres they cannot understand? Set questions as per model	4
16	To what extent are UK nationals naturally friendly towards their foreign counterparts? Do they tend to develop real friendships even in business relatively quickly? Are they not very much concerned with embarrassment or loss of face?	4
17	To what extent is the community in UK relatively informal about how people deal with one another? For example, to what extent does the community avoid laying down rules and codes of behaviour about how you dress or speak (to superiors or subordinates) or act (bowing with deference and respect, for example to a superior)? Is impoliteness sometimes seen as acceptable?	3
18	To what extent do people in UK seem to have a natural tendency towards impatience and decisiveness? Do they always want to get on with things? Do they tend to be restive with a lot of debate about what to do? Do they usually want quick results, reckoning that actions speak louder than words?	3

Average = 3.5

Britain prides itself on being an open society. However the global security situation and large scale immigration has resulted in destabilising that model.

Britain can thus be assessed as having a generally IMO culture – somewhat **I**ndividualist, somewhat **M**aterialistic and somewhat **O**pen in nature. This represents a western society generally satisfied with its way of life although feeling itself under pressure.

When the results are placed onto two overlapping triangles we see that both nations are not too far apart except when it comes to Bedrock Culture. So, what else is there about the way China and UK see their social environment that causes such frequent confusion and frustration on both sides?

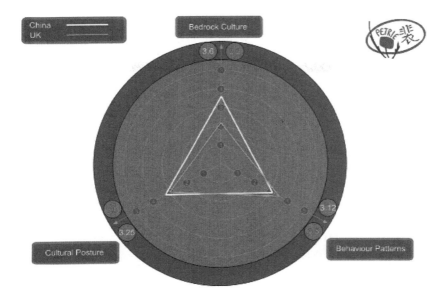

The Triangle Test Instrument for China and the UK
(adapted from Terry Garrison)

The Dragon awakes – Communism

Let us remind ourselves of some recent history. For China the 20th Century was a period of civil strife even after Chairman Mao Zedong's Communist Red Army beat General Jiang Kai-shek's Nationalist forces in 1949. There were internal political campaigns such as the Hundred Flowers Movement 百花齐放，百家争鸣 (bǎihuǎ qīfàng, bǎijiā zhēngmíng) – this translates as 'Let a hundred flowers blossom and a hundred schools of thought contend') when Mao initially sought to promote the progress of arts and sciences in developing China's Socialist culture during the 1950s; this however misfired and resulted in twenty years of oppression after the criticisms of the intellectuals became unacceptably strident. The Revolutionary fervour of the Great Leap Forward 大跃进 (Dàyuèjìn) followed with Socialist prosperity as its main aim. The country was mobilized, huge construction projects were begun, fields were overplanted and every piece of metal was smelted down. Great hardship resulted and relations with the USSR were badly damaged. These ties with the former USSR go back a long way with many senior Chinese speaking excellent Russian from their student days.

Further calamity followed in 1966 with the Great Proletarian Cultural Revolution 文化大革命 (Wénhuá dàgémíng) as Mao struggled to maintain power. Battalions of students roamed the country as his loyal Red Guards fighting rival units and destroying anything or anyone which challenged Mao's thoughts as set out in his famous Little Red Book 红宝书 (Hóngbǎoshū). This tumult only ended in 1976 when Mao died. This was a sad and bloody end to a reign which had reunified China after the decline of the Manchurian Qing Emperors and had set it on the path to international acceptance. In two key areas Mao restored pride – to the nation and to her people. For individuals, the legacy was very much in accordance with the old Chinese proverb that it is the nail standing proud above the rest that gets hammered flat, or as the influential Duke Zhou wrote, the straightest tree is the first to be cut down – to this day there is still a residual reluctance to stand out from the crowd. Not only in terms of individualism but also in terms of wider mindset, communism is remains a powerful influence. Take for instance the regard for layers of administration and the liking for referring decisions back to higher authority for which the alert visiting businesswoman or man must always be prepared.

The new Chinese mindset – Capitalism

A more pragmatic period began with Chairman's Mao's passing. One of his compatriots on the legendary 6,000-mile Long March in 1934-35 was Deng Xiaoping 邓小平 (Dèng Xiǎopíng). The Communists fled from Jiangxi Province 江西省 (Jiāngxi shěng) to safety in Shaanxi Province 陕西省 (Shǎnxī shěng)where the Communists sought to escape annihilation at the hands of the Nationalists. This heroic trek across some of China's most inhospitable areas bred a cadre of future Chinese leaders and Deng was one such hero. He and his family, however, suffered cruelly during the Cultural Revolution for his modern and pragmatic views but with Mao's death he was able to position himself and China for catching up with the West. Through such initiatives as the Four Modernizations 四个现代化 (Sìge xiàndàihuà) in which agriculture, defence, industry and science were formally recognized as key areas needing urgent and expert attention, not just the enthusiastic mobilization of the masses if China was to win through. Another of Deng's most relevant legacies to Western business was the establishment of the Special Economic Zones – SEZs or 经济特区 (Jīngjìtèqū). They are exactly what they sound like, special geographical areas selected for economic development and administered in such a way as to attract foreign investment with tax breaks and favourable tariffs, etc.

These moves were not achieved without opposition, but the one-time Capitalist Roaders had their way as we all know. Today's China is confident, capable and credible in commercial terms worldwide. The Chinese, always traders and negotiators, now have undreamt of personal freedom in all respects save in politics, have seized on the late Deng's exhortation "To be rich is glorious" with a fervour that has excited us all. They have a very clear idea of where they are heading and increasingly are learning from the West just how to get there. A new generation of leaders is in place continuing to lead China's socialist modernization but has fuelled concern that growth may run out of control and has already split the wealthy eastern seaboard and the rest of the nation. This explains in one way the severe response to the student demonstrations in Tiananmen Square, when development was moving too fast and also, by demonstrating over official corruption in the universities, a serious challenge had been offered to the Party. It was not helpful that the Soviet leader, Gorbachev was on a State Visit to Beijing at the time.

ABC analysis

In wishing to delve further into this fascinating issue Melville Petrie devised the 'ABC Test' because previous research had revealed the powerful effect the way people reacted to **Artefacts**, how they **Behaved** towards one another and the way they **Communicated** in all manner of ways. By plotting those on the following wheel, which quickly became dubbed the Cultural Jellyfish, one can see at a glance where one group of people differ from another in their responses on the three key dimensions.

The interested reader can check Appendix 2 to look in detail at the questionnaires but for those with less time the key findings follow.

The indicative date from the Test responses were answered on a scale from 1 – "I disagree entirely with this proposition or statement" – through to 10 – "I agree totally with this proposition or statement". Use was made of '0' to indicate a 'non' response since primary data was used.

Artefacts

The results were plotted to show the areas of convergence and divergence in the diagram below and when we look into the detail of the responses we can see that as regards Artefacts, there is general agreement across the results except in so far as national flags are concerned.

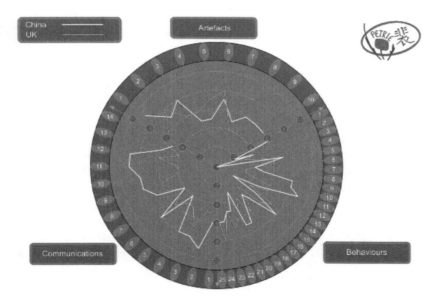

ABC Analysis Model
(Melville Petrie®)

Although at present, with the London Olympics the British may be feeling rather more patriotic than usual, a succession of increasingly unpopular wars has reduced UK jingo-ism and so whilst they score a positive '6' in relations to national flags, the Chinese score this a '9' and overall their scores in support of objects of status are slightly higher.

The Chinese see things like flags and uniforms in a much more relevant and enthusiastic way than do we. As a culture in which people traditionally have seen themselves only in relation to their family or local group they have sought confirming artefacts to show that they belong and to which group. The Scots do exactly the same thing with their family or nowadays corporate, sports team or association tartans. Flags, emblems and badges are regarded as highly important and it pays to respect them in China.

There is great leverage in this as well for the enterprising western company. Some chose to localize their product offerings by showing a Chinese element in their corporate logo, such as Jardine Matheson, the great Hong Kong trading house. They made their Scottish credentials clear by using the national plant, the thistle, as their emblem but has their Chinese name, in Cantonese, Yee Wo within its bud. Others choose to differentiate themselves as an aspirational product with a logo redolent of their own culture. The British International School in Shanghai is parented from the UK and proudly boasts an armorial coat of arms with Latin motto to set itself apart from any competition so as to reassure discerning parents. The Chinese tend to attune immediately to any logo and will then scrutinize it deeply.

Showing more than passing respect to the red national flag of China with its gold stars or even to company flags and corporate logos will always gain you the advantage. There are two reasons for this. On the one hand you are showing respect to the artefact in the same way as your host and also you are showing respect for them in respecting their customs. In the same way, receiving business cards with respect is critical and we will return to cards later.

Behaviours

The drive to get rich has had a profound effect on the Chinese. More and more they think very individualistically and this can throw Westerners brought up with a traditional view of the East. Young Chinese have their MBAs, they are smart in IT skills and they want what they see on their television and computer screens, now, and are impatient for change. Although the important elements producing China's Bedrock Culture remain very different from those determining European cultures, such is the power of the new and the general focus on achieving individual success and wealth that the visiting business person should constantly remind him or herself of China's recent past. This past influences the way the capable and tough-talking Chinese executive in discussion with you is actually thinking. In short, without a grasp of the nature of the land and her people, many vital messages will be missed. The playing field is getting more and more even, but it is still the Western businesswoman or man who understands China and her people who succeeds. A useful example of this would be to learn a few key facts about Chinese history so that you can let your hosts know this and so gain respect, or Face, or Mianzi .

One can see from this test that the Chinese see it as far less important than the British to have a wide circle of friends extending beyond one's immediate work group and that they find greater pleasure in mixing with work colleagues away from the workplace. The Chinese reveal themselves as attaching much more importance to the whole matter of and regard for business cards so closely are these essential business tools aligned to Face. As a developing nation it is interesting to note the much higher importance they accord to the equitable treatment of foreign business women and perhaps this is as much a consequence of fresh realization of ladies' capabilities as a softening of traditionally strongly male attitudes. It is important for British businessmen and women to be aware that fraudulent paperwork still has a place in Asian business and whilst responding in a lukewarm fashion to this question, British business people now need to be alive to the personal implications of the *UK Bribery Act* wherever they are – all in all this is a surprising result. Given the occasionally onerous nature of friendships and obligation across Asia, one would expect to see that the Chinese score much more highly in this dimension and this is an area which foreign businessmen – waishang – need to be careful of as both side's expectations are very different.

Communications

Change is everywhere in China, from the rich coastal cities of the east to the remote hinterlands to the north, west, and south. People are becoming wealthier, have access to better education and opportunities than ever before but at heart the traditional structure of society is being maintained by her people continuing to favour strongly formal ways of communicating – be it in conversation, what they regard as appropriate (and highly effective) negotiating skills, using foreign languages or in setting out business letters.   This accords fully with the order and balance traditionally encouraged by Confucius, the Legalist school and Communism. Do not be misled, this business world is still moving ahead at breakneck speed despite this respect for formality!

The Communications' results show both interesting differences between the two nations and changes within UK. Good manners appear to be valued equally until the matter of discussions is looked into and in spite of negotiations in China being very much a role-play affair where pretty much anything goes, the British are very much less concerned about causing offence in discussion. UK companies often get caught out in China when a first contract is signed and do not see it as merely a preliminary agreement for further negotiations. Unsurprisingly, the British come over as less than enthusiastic about the value of speaking foreign languages in business, while the Chinese with their economic success rate this a '9' and trust their interpreters much more – in all likelihood because they will normally provide them. Business has got tougher over the years and both value guile as a weapon.

Case Study – Right Flag, Wrong Flag

A visit to a Western warship by a very senior Chinese admiral quickly deteriorated into a diplomatic incident not many years ago. Normal marks of respect paid to foreign naval VIPs visiting a warship include the ceremonial unfurling of the visitor's national flag amid bands playing and an armed guard of honour. All went very well on this occasion as the distinguished guest was ushered onto the flight deck of the huge vessel. It was a great honour for the ship and her captain to have such a visitor and also there was a lot of curiosity about the man since visits to the west by the Peoples' Liberation Army's Navy are very rare. Disaster struck when the flag hoisted was not the red and gold flag of the People's Republic of China but the blue, red and white flag of her disputatious neighbour, the Republic of China – Taiwan. So insulted was the Chinese admiral by the complete, although unintentional and unwanted, slur that he stormed off the aircraft carrier's flight deck, down the many decks to the quayside and into his limousine. It then took a very long time and considerable placatory effort by his hosts to coax him from his fastness and back on board. Memories are long in China and such slights may be forgiven but never, ever, forgotten. (The North Korean reaction to their Southern neighbour's flag being hoisted during the London Olympics instead of their own was equally grave.

ABC in context

By way of review, Chinese society is in transition and where the big shift is first occurring is in the realm of the individual who is taking every opportunity to shape his or her own future as controls are eased by their Government as it seeks to increase China's prosperity. The notion of individual sense of identity being bound up almost exclusively within the context of immediate family, childhood friends, village, university, work or PLA unit is being replaced very rapidly by an individualism best exemplified in the USA whose recent history has been created by generations of immigrant pioneers seeking their fortune. Artefacts remain highly important, as does formality in communications, but in the realm of behaviour the Chinese increasingly now see themselves as in the western individualistic mould and that is where we must focus.

4

PHILOSOPHY AND RELIGION IN CHINA

Religion and philosophy in China have been characterised by pluralism. Taoism, Buddhism, Confucianism have coexisted for centuries, and ancestor worship is a theme that transcends all.

Taoism

Taoism is a philosophical and religious tradition that emphasizes living in harmony. The philosophical Taoism, individualistic by nature, is not institutionalized. It synthesize the concepts of Yin-Yang 阴阳 (Yīnyáng) and the Five Elements – the Wu Xing 五行 (Wǔháng). The Tao 道 (Dào) means a way, path or principle, it denotes something that is both the source and the driving force behind everything that exists in the world. Wuwei 无为 (wúwéi) means that to do nothing is actually to do everything. The Taoism suggests that humans must obey the law of nature and should not put incessant demands on Nature itself. So it has become a mainstream concept in the traditional Chinese outlook on the world – to 'obey the laws of Nature and follow human desire.' It is also an important ideological cornerstone of the architecture of being Chinese.

As a religion, it believes in ghosts and spirits and emphasised cooperation with the natural forces. Taoists advocate a life of simplicity, and encourage their followers to perform good deeds, and seek inner peace through the cultivation of optimism, passivity, and inner calm, and to show compassion, moderation, and humility. Going with the flow and accepting things as they happen rather than pursuing power and wealth are important concepts in Taoism.

The Book of Tao and its virtues 道德经 (Dàodéjīng) by Lao Zi 老子 (Lǎozi) (770 b.c.), together with the writings of Zhuangzi 庄子 (Zhuāngzi) (369-286 b.c.), are the philosophical foundation of Taoism.

Laozi, a native of Chu, lived during the Zhou dynasty (in modern Henan province) according to the record in the Shiji 史记 (Shǐjì). Laozi served as an archival record keeper at the Court of Zhou.

Zhuangzi was a minor official from the town of Meng (in modern Anhui province) in the state of Song. Zhuangzi is the most significant of China's early interpreters of Taoism.

Taoism has had a profound influence on Chinese culture that continues to this day. People will do everything to maintain harmony with one another and achieve consonance with nature. People continue to follow traditional Taoism's guide to live their lives: obey their elders, love their parents, be tolerant, help others, practice self-control of mind and body, and be selfless.

Art of War

The Art of War – Sunzi's Military Principles 孙子兵法 (Sūnzǐ bīngfǎ) is an ancient Chinese military treatise by Sunzi 孙子 (Sūnzǐ) (476-221 b.c.). It advised firstly the use of strategies and then diplomacy to defeat the enemy. These were then followed by invasion, and lastly laying siege to the enemy's cities and castles. His work, *The Art of War*, is universally regarded as a classic, not only treasured by military, but also in the diplomatic and business worlds.

Sunzi was born around 500 b.c. and was a contemporary of Confucius. A second "Art of War" was written by Sunbin about 100 years later. Sunbin was said to be a descendant of Sunzi.

Sunzi and Sunbin considered war as a necessary evil that should be avoided whenever possible. They believed that war is like fire and people who do not lay down their arms will die by their arms. War should be fought swiftly to avoid economic losses as no long war ever profited any country. Anyone who excels in defeating his enemies triumphs before his enemy's threat become real. Winning without fighting is the best and an important thought in ancient Chinese military theory. The golden rule of a war is that massacres should be avoided at all cost because this can provoke resistance and possibly allow enemy to turn the war in his favour. The real victor will capture a state intact, and win the enemy over.

Sunzi emphasises the importance of positioning in military strategy. The decision to position an army must be based on both objective conditions in the physical environment and the subjective beliefs of other, competitive actors in that environment. He explored the five fundamental factors: the way, seasons, terrain, leadership, and management and method that determine the outcomes of military engagements. By thinking, assessing and comparing these points, a commander can calculate his chances of victory. He explains how to understand the economy of warfare, and how success requires winning decisive engagements quickly. The intelligence-gathering process focuses on the importance of developing good information sources.

The Chinese have a philosophy of war that values victory without battles because their history gives them a deep understanding of war and a clear assessment of its consequences.

Buddhism in China

Buddhism was first introduced to China from India and reached its highest point at the Tang Dynasty, when it was repressed because of its association with individuals withdrawing from their social obligations. Buddhism is a belief and practice based on principles of compassion and non-attachment. The Buddhist believes in sudden enlightenment by focusing on the suppression of passions. It says a person must release all desire to reach a state of liberation and freedom from all suffering. All actions have consequences. Actions in this and earlier lifetimes will be felt in the next one, in a process known as reincarnation.

Buddhists were not free of persecution, especially by Confucian-oriented statesmen. Many people converted and entered a monastery to escape military service and taxpaying. Repression started under the Taoist Emperor Wuzong in the Tang Dynasty and the revival of Confucianism under the Song Dynasty continued the decline of

Buddhism as a state religion. However, as popular belief, Buddhism is still very widespread, but highly mixed with Taoist belief.

Over China's long history, Buddhism has left an indelible impact on Chinese civilization, literature, language, art, science and people's way of thinking. This is particularly so on the western side of China were the number of Buddhist followers is at its densest. The ideas, such as impermanence and suffering, karma and rebirth, paradises and hells, emptiness and reality, bondage and liberation, are all essential to the development of Chinese literary thoughts. For example, the famous poets Tao Yuanming 陶渊明 (Táo Yuānmíng), Wang Wei 王维 (Wáng Wéi), Bai Juyi 白居易 (Bái Jūyì) and Su Shi 苏轼 (Sū Shì) are obviously influenced by the thoughts of Buddhism. Many words and phrases have root in a Buddhist origin. For an example, 'to hold the foot of Buddha at the moment' means to make a last minute effort. This reveals a sense of the utilitarian attitude of the Chinese toward belief systems. Buddhism and its symbols (like dragons and chopsticks) are still very much part of the Chinese culture. The Laughing Buddha ("Pot-Belly Buddha") is the transformation of an Indian skete into a deity objectifying Chinese ideals. Most people still believe in 'Karma' and Chinese vegetarianism relates to Buddhists' compassion and respect for life.

In today's China, Buddhist temples, Buddhist caves and Buddhist Holy Mountains, especially the ones listed in the national or provincial historical and cultural relics, have become hot spots for tourism.

Confucianism

Confucianism is a Chinese ethical and philosophical belief system based on the teaching of Kongfuzi 孔夫子 (Kǒng Fūzǐ), 551-478 b.c. Kongzi was born in 551 B.C. in the State of Lu (in modern Qufu, Shandong province) to a minor aristocratic family. His father died when he was three, he was raised by his mother in poverty. He was fortunate to receive an education. After his studies he went back to this hometown, worked as a shepherd, cowherd, clerk, and a book-keeper. At the height of his career, Confucius reached the growing class of shi 士 (shì), intermediate between the aristocracy and the common people. He lived in a time of great conflict and continual civil war. He was exiled from the Shi post at age of 50, began journeying around the small kingdoms of northeast and central China, and started preaching good moral conduct. He died in exile at the age of 73. None of the courts at which he expounded his beliefs, seem to have been implemented them. He was not particularly interested in religion, except insofar as it related to social life.

The Five Classics and Four Books of Confucianism of philosophy served as the basis of the Chinese education system for centuries. His doctrine and principles were established into the Chinese Law in 210 b.c. Most of the original texts for his writings were destroyed during the Qin Dynasty. What remains is mostly records by his students or interpretation by later followers. Crucially, ancient Chinese civil service exams were based on the Confucian thoughts and students were required to study his works over the 6 centuries between 1313 and 1905. In fact, regardless of social background anyone could advance by exams, a belief that is still held by many in China today. After Confucius died in 479 b.c. his followers built temples and erected beautiful monuments in his honour across China.

Tomb of Confucius in Kong Lin Cemetery, Qufu, Shandong Province

The mainstream ideal society of China was and is seen as a world of many individuals acting rationally, organized around a series of societal orders in a great harmony. Etiquette and benevolence are integral to the social theories of Confucius. He taught that a set of orders and norms must be established for life. From the top ruler, to his ministers, to fathers and to sons, everyone must behave in a manner appropriate to his position and follow an ordained set of rules and guidelines. No word may be uttered, nor any behaviour contemplated, in breach of these rules and guidelines. The Confucian idea of filial piety and the compassion of the ruler for his subjects are very similar to Buddhism.

The early sages in China believed that the family was the basic element of society. Since a family is bonded through blood, the relationship between father and son is the core of the relationship. This relationship is extended further, to encompass relationships between husband and wife, monarch and the subject, senior and junior and between friends. These are the Five Cardinal Relationships, and they cover most of the relationships between people in a society. Confucius held benevolence to be the highest standard of social ethics and the nation's moral benchmark, especially when its wellbeing was at stake. He hoped that his thinking would become the moral code for the Chinese people.

Mencius 孟子 (Mèngzǐ), 372-289 b.c., a Chinese philosopher, was one of the principal interpreters of Confucianism and a pupil of Confucius' grandson.

He raised the notion of righteousness as the core value and the supreme standard of ethics. His five fundamental moral principles were benevolence, righteousness, courtesy, intelligence and faith. Righteousness implies justice and moral principles and upholding it remains one of the essential moral standards for the Chinese.

Confucius believed people are equal at birth, teachable, improvable and perfectible through personal and communal endeavour. A peaceful solution to life's turmoil could come through the practice of veneration of one's ancestors and respect for one's elders. Education was seen as a means of producing virtuousness, and trustworthy people would be able to govern for the good of all. Conflict is defined as the upset of the social order and harmony must be preserved under social norms, relationships and in families.

Confucian ethics are characterised by the promotion of virtues, encompassed by the Five Constants, or the Wuchang 五常 (Wǔcháng):

- Ren 仁 (Rén): Benevolence, humanity
- Yi 仪 (Yí): righteousness, the moral disposition to do good.
- Li 礼 (Lǐ): principle of gain, benefit; in general, 'principle', propriety, ritual, social order.
- Zhi 智 (Zhì): Knowledge
- Xin 信 (Xìn): Integrity.

These are accompanied by the classical Four Virtues 四字 (Sìzì):

- Zhong 忠 (Zhōng): loyalty, faithful, and devoted
- Xiao 孝 (Xiào): filial piety
- Jie 节 (Jié): human heartedness, humaneness
- Yi 义 (Yì): Righteousness.

There are still many other elements.

- Jing 敬 (Jìng): filial piety, reverence and familial love
- De 德 (Dé): virtue, moral, mind and kindness.

Among all elements, Ren and Yi are fundamental.

Chinese people still like to maintain societal order and harmony, as there is a place for everyone and everyone does know their place – status and hierarchy. Good human relationship with family, ruler and friends – guanxi 关系 (guānxì) – does matter. Confucianism preaches diligence and obedience, and people still maintain certain rituals in communication. People suppress their own personal needs for their families. Confucius's teaching on scholarship, although possibly effecting Chinese the most, also influence South Korea, Japan and Singapore. Through learning you can rise in society. If people's behaviour is inappropriate in a given situation, it will causes loss of Face and the destruction of harmony.

Popular folk religion

Popular religion has been dismissed as superstition by the Chinese Government since the Chinese communists came into power in 1949, yet the various folk traditions of the rural masses have continued a preoccupation with other worldly concerns.

Ancestor worship 中国民间宗教 or 信仰 (Zhōngguó mínjiān zōngjiào or xìnyǎng) involves rituals, devotional worship, festivals and various other practices associated with different folk gods and goddesses that form an important part of Chinese culture today. Chinese people offer prayers and food, light incense sticks and make burnt paper offerings for their ancestors. These activities are typically conducted at the site of ancestral graves or tombs, a temple, or household shrine. The family cult relates to ancestors and to family events such as birth, marriage and death. Families will combine elements from Buddhism, Daoism and Confucianism, since none of these makes claims of exclusivity. There is much semi-magical and superstitious belief mixed in with more overtly religious elements.

Conclusion

It has often been said that the Chinese are not deeply religious. However, Chinese people often follow the teachings of Confucius when they were successful in life, turn to Taoism when things are difficult and frustrating and pray to Buddha when facing a very hard time. It is nonetheless true that they have shown a comparative indifference to metaphysical speculation. Chinese culture was perhaps the first to develop an intellectual scepticism concerning the gods. Many people never read the Buddhist sutras but would say they believe in gods, destiny, fate, luck and an afterlife. In real life people will make decisions by themselves or resort to either family or friends for help, rather than rely on prayer. Ancestor worship has been a key element in all China's traditions. If you lose "Face" it is a loss to your family, to your clan and your heritage. This is manifested in a complex mix of religious, superstitious and magical beliefs and practices.

In their different ways most Chinese have shown themselves to be concerned primarily with the human person and society. In a predominantly rural country, this has manifested itself in a concern for the land and its prosperity.

In last twenty years or so, most faiths and beliefs have started enjoying a renaissance since the Chinese Government eased its policy against religions.

5

WHAT THE CHINESE THINK OF WESTERNERS

中国 (Zhōngguó) – The Middle Kingdom

The term Middle Kingdom is not just a romantic and exciting way to translate China's name into English, it is also extremely telling in reading the minds of her people. Because of her 6,000-year recorded history the bedrock mass of culture lead the Chinese to see themselves as innately superior to other nations less culturally fortunate than themselves. The newcomer to this land of infinite fascination quickly learns to recognize that the Chinese all see themselves, be they street-sweepers in squalid, crowded city streets or prosperous entrepreneurs being driven around in their sleek black cars, as natives of a nation halfway between Earth and Heaven. All societies are unique and the Chinese are brought up from infancy and through the educational system to regard being Chinese as more unique than anyone else. The Middle Kingdom is halfway between Heaven and Earth. This world picture, as you would imagine, impacts significantly on how they interact with foreigners.

But how then do these innately elevated beings regard Westerners? Or is thus just an illusion? Although there are many more passports issued in China than in the past, the vast majority of Chinese have only come into contact with the west through films and television. This has given them a very slanted picture. They see a world where everyone is rich and well-dressed, people change their clothes ten times a day with the assistance of immigrant maids, women lack morality and spend more time with their *inamorato* than their children, and where children are thrown out of the family home at 18 so weak are the family ties. If however, you view China from the standpoint of their 19th Century subjugation by Western powers with the deep sense of history all Chinese share, then you can see an underlying unease with foreigners. No wonder our cultures clash and no wonder we are difficult to understand when we fail to align to our Hollywood stereotypes.

Right now, white Westerners are the most favoured race beneath the Chinese in this view of the world. Next to them come the immensely influential ethnic Chinese investors from the wider Chinese diaspora around the Pacific Rim and further afield. Those from the Middle East and Indian Sub-continent come next and finally, ethnic Africans. In an intrinsically dualist way, the Chinese see nothing contradictory in setting themselves up as leaders of the Third World and yet holding its people in low regard as they forge ahead in their development of Africa's natural resources and resettle many of their own people there. This discrimination is largely economic rather than racial. Whilst this approach reflects Chinese memory of being treated thus when they were poor and subservient to Westerners after "The Unequal Treaties" were imposed upon them in the 19th Century, it also follows the long tradition of Chinese exploitation of its neighbours in prior centuries. Similarly, the deep divisions still felt between Japan and China have recently resurfaced over a group of disputed islands. When Japan's economy was buoyant the issue was manageable but now that China is in the ascendancy, any perceived insult to their territorial integrity can and has been robustly dealt with.

This perspective currently opens many doors of opportunity for ethnic Caucasians but sadly poses significant obstacles in the way of ethnically diverse Britons attempting to do the same. Hopefully, these attitudes will soften as China continues to open up to the outside world.

19th Century and 20th Century experiences of the West

These contradictions are in many ways the result of China's humiliation at the hands of the West in the 19th and 20th Centuries. At those times the country had closed its doors on the outside world and ceased to build on the exploration and advances made in previous centuries when their ships traded with Oman and beyond. Westerners such as the Butterfields, Dents, Jardines, Mathesons and Swires grasped the enormous opportunities presented by trading cotton and opium with China and taking silks, porcelain and tea back to a western market hungry for chinoiserie of all sorts. Ports of choice included Shanghai 上海 (Shànghǎi), Amoy or Xiamen 厦门 (Xiàmén), Canton or Guangzhou 广州 (Guǎnghzhōu) and Hong Kong 香港 (Xiānggǎng). Fabulous fortunes were amassed and conglomerates of huge and continuing significance established – you will still see some of their names in China to this day. Due to a combination of the insularity of the Qing Dynasty, its arrogance, national backwardness and the overwhelming military might of the West a whole series of Unequal Treaties were imposed on China following the Opium Wars in the 19th Century. The memories of these humiliations linger amongst a people steeped in their history. In short, they see little reason to trust foreigners – one only has to look at what happened to China not so long ago. However, the Chinese are great pragmatists – think only of the horrors committed by the Japanese army in Nanjing during 1937 and then of the tremendous trade that now goes on between the two nations.

Industrial and commercial revolutions

This really is that the Chinese do admire the West and what it has achieved for its peoples. They by no means wish to be British or American but each and every one is hungry to have the benefits of the wealth that they see portrayed in the global media, be what the hip young seen on MTV or more traditional stars from Hollywood or British films. Their own Industrial Revolution is happening in a matter of years and they are immensely proud of their progress.

Western politics

The Chinese have a real difficulty with politics as practised in the West. Not only do the politicians, the senior Communist Party of China cadres, find liberalism in any form disconcerting at best and downright dangerous at worst, but also the ordinary people, the 老百姓 (lǎobǎixìng) (the old one hundred names), find much of it strangely irrelevant. They now have so much more freedom than ever before and they have the opportunity to make money and like their southern neighbours in Hong Kong largely aspire to be left in peace to prosper. The last British Governor of Hong Kong, Geoffrey Paton, created turmoil in the Colony by endeavouring to introduce a degree of western-style democracy, never embarked on during the 100 years of colonial government, but attempted immediately prior to hand over to China regardless. It was, however, largely unwanted by the majority of the local people who were preparing in their own and very different ways for their Communist brothers and sisters to come across the border. There was, for example, already a significant mainland police presence working with the Royal Hong Kong Police so that each could learn what worked and what did not in the two nations. The UK and other western nations were lobbied for passports with differing degrees of success. Hong Kong being Hong Kong, business continued with the commercial arms of the People's Liberation Army learning the ways of western property speculation in Hong Kong years before Handover in June 1997. In Mainland China, the standard of living had begun to rise fast and today's inflation had yet to become a harsh fact of life for the new PRC middle class. In fact in the authors' home town in Gloucestershire, the lady owner of a Chinese gift shop bemoans the fact that for all her hard work, it is her sister back home in Guangzhou who has a far better life style and fewer domestic maintenance problems!

Personal freedom

The issue of personal freedom can be desperately sensitive for both those brought up in the individualistic and materialistic West and those from the traditionally corporatist and communitarian East where such philosophies are seen as selfish and immature. Even the stereotypical Chinese duality has difficulty in rationalizing its stance on personal freedom. Having been told by Deng that "poverty was not socialism" and that "to be rich was glorious" today's Chinese have a huge balancing act to manage. Finding a good job is as tough in China as anywhere. To make it to the big time needs connections 关系 (guānxì), capital, ability, good fortune and the ability to skip from pinnacle to pinnacle of success (perhaps ignoring the rule of law). In short, you are unlikely to make it as a member of the crowd. You need to be a pretty focused loner, working in parallel to rather than within the normal retinue of close associates and friends. You have to conduct business rather like a Westerner whilst remaining Chinese. Many have made fortunes in just this way.

Case Study – Broad Group

Mr Zhang Yue, President of Broad Group, or Yuanda 远大 (yuándà), founded his business in 1988 at the age of 26 with his brother, with ¥30,000, or about £2,500, in his home town of Changsha 长沙 (Chǎngshā). Eschewing Communist Party membership, he developed highly sophisticated air conditioning systems using pollution-free absorption chiller technology. Passionate not only about his products but globally eclectic, when it came to building his own management school, that was constructed in the grand style of Versailles and the grounds are populated by life-size bronze statues of luminaries such as GE's Jack Welch, Deng Xiaoping and Albert Einstein plus a full-size pyramid. Independent throughout, he was the first person in China to own a private helicopter. All is not personal aggrandizement as a slogan on one of the factory's dormitories reads "Improve yourself". All is not "all work and no play" for his workers as they are allowed to see their families at weekends. All new employees have to complete a week-long boot camp training but Mr Zhang sees this as essential to turning workers into loyal followers. This is key to him as, in common with many other wealthy entrepreneurs, the need to change individual mindsets away from command economy autonomism is critical to commercial success. Zhang Yue's sense of design and environmental contribution with his non-electrical air-conditioning and the Broad Sustainable Building construction technique has been recognized by the UN Environment Programme's Champion of the Earth Award for fighting climate change (China Daily August 21, 2012). Readers should cast their minds back to Yingshi's previous chapter on Chinese Philosophy and Religion to think just what Zhang Yue has laid to one side in securing his fortune.

Western wealth

Western wealth is admired, envied and to some extent feared by the Chinese. Wealth has brought comfort, health, happiness and great pride to the rich West. Because that is no fantasy limited to the media but attainable, apparently by all, this is where today's Chinese want to be. However, until securely in that Western state of bliss, the very power which the riches bring, make the West a force to be treated, if not with respect, then with some caution. And, most importantly, as a resource into which the Chinese feel uniquely entitled to tap. One of the greatest difficulties every foreign businessman or woman has to overcome is the assumption, that by merely arriving in China, one is immediately and unquestioningly, a source of free foreign investment/currency and know-how. Even though there are over 960,000 Chinese US$ millionaires, as reported by Trippon, these are still a tiny minority and for most of their countrymen and women life remains hard. Generally under 40 years old and 30% female, they remain confused as what to do with this wealth. That has given birth to a whole service industry in China which introduces this new swathe of high net worth individuals to suitable retailers of accoutrements suitable to the status they are keen to flaunt and so gain in Face.

Western know-how

Your Chinese business partner will, beyond a shadow of a doubt, appear to regard herself or himself as innately superior to you, as a newcomer to an infinitely more worthy society. However, they will have a huge regard for whatever know-how you bring with you. Provided you treat your business partners with respect any underlining insecurity dating from historically bad treatment by foreigners of the Chinese nation will not surface. The continuing progress and development of the West is a source of great interest to China. They are interested in just how we have managed to pull this off consistently since the Industrial Revolution began in the second half of the 18th Century. They are keen to do just the same themselves and have begun with staggering success over the last quarter century. Never underestimate the negotiating power of offers of 'technological' transfer and be careful it does not happen beyond your control. As Yingshi has pointed out, the Chinese do not believe that anyone can own an idea. Once you have mastered that idea, it is yours to use. The way ahead is continual updating accompanied by constant vigilance.

6

BUSINESS BASICS IN CHINA

Being taken seriously

One of the greatest frustrations of establishing oneself in China is in being regarded as just another transient visitor with no long-term interest in the nation. The whole Chinese mindset sets everything in relation to its own historical and economic perspective and that extends as much into the future as much as it reaches back into the past when it comes to establishing relevance. It is not impossible to be taken seriously in China, but it takes thought, planning and time – and, good Joss!

Commitment and trust

The first thing that your Chinese counterparts will be looking to find in your corporate approach to doing business with them is tangible evidence of commitment to a long-term business relationship. This relationship they will wish to be based on a least equal profitability and significant transfer, be it of skills, technology or finance to China. This slightly unequal perspective is deep in the Chinese mind whereas the western 'win-win' model is not. The nation has been brought up on millennia of market haggling overlaid with subjugation by foreigners and they feel it their right to take a robust stand with all *waiguoren*. Whereas one of the greatest compliments that can be paid to a Chinese businessperson is 八面玲珑 (bāmiàn línglóng) – eight faces and slippery – they will not accept the same from you, because as we have already seen, the West still owes China. What will really make your Chinese partners comfortable is involvement in your corporate strategic planning and firm evidence that you will stay in China. Assigning executives in China and regular and reciprocal visits by senior management between the two head offices can demonstrate this last very forcibly.

Business cards

Right across Asia, business cards are a vital artefact to doing business. The quality of the card used and the information that it carries all set out how you are perceived, and in China, your actual status where job titles are 'king'. B-schools in Asia tell their students to expect to be general managers or VPs by their mid-twenties and the business cards reflect this.

The exchange of business card is expected at any initial introduction for a business meeting in China. Having your business card translated professionally and printed in good quality card is a worthwhile investment. Rebranding your business for the Chinese market place means adopting a Chinese name and that is an art. Your personal and company name translations can be phonetic sounds using certain commonly used neutral words for the closest pronunciation, for example, McDonald's (the earliest imported fast food chain in China) is translated directly into Chinese as 麦当劳 (Mài dāng láo). 麦当劳 does not mean anything apart from the similarity in sound. This is the easiest and most common way to translate a name to Chinese.

A second way is to select a real Chinese name showing aspects of femininity, masculinity, good health, fortune, integrity, success, kindness, love and affection, etc. So you can base yours on the image or philosophy you would like to project to people in your new market by choosing appropriate positive Chinese characters to give a more meaningful translation. This may not sound quite the same. For example Britain's Jaguar car brand in Chinese is 捷豹 (Jié bào) literally 'the victorious, triumphant, quick, nimble and prompt wild jaguar'.

The Chinese name given to my co-author picks up on his surname of Petrie using 裴 (Péi) and his first name, Melville as 茂荣 (Máoróng) to send messages of wealth, profusion and honour, so 裴茂荣 (Péi Máoróng).

Actually, the best way is to combine sound and positive-meaning words, for example Subway (a recent importer of fast food). The Chinese name is 赛百味 (Sài bǎi wèi), literally 'better-than hundreds of tastes' which sound close to the original English, and the meaning is much better. Please see the language section for more information on how to do this.

Your personal name, job title (which helps people understand where you fit in your company's hierarchy) company name and company address should be in English on one side and on the reverse in Chinese. In translating job titles, remember that the choice of characters will determine how you are regarded; company structures may be different in China. Be careful, your business card must use simplified Chinese characters and not the traditional, full characters which are still used in Taiwan and some south-east Asian countries.

Colour schemes on the card can be same as on the English side of the card, or you may want to have something in the auspicious red or gold but never in green because of its negative sexual connotations. If, for corporate branding reasons, you really must have green then balance it red. Fonts matter too. Whereas in the West we like a card to look elegant, in China, names and company names need to look bolder.

There is a whole tradition that has grown up around business cards and how they should be presented. Although in recent years business cards can be exchanged in the Western way with just one hand, the preferred, polite way is to use both hands. The Chinese place great store by these vital commercial artefacts. You are laying your soul bare by them. They proclaim not only who you are but also your actual and perceived status.

On meeting someone for the first time, present your card with both hands, Chinese side up, the typeface facing the recipient so that the recipient can easily read it. Receive a card in the same way and examine the card carefully paying extra attention to the job title and surname, so that you know how to address him/her (surname plus job title, for example: Manager Wang 王经理 (Wáng jīnglǐ)), before putting the card in a proper business card case. Be careful, never write on someone's card unless directed to do so, and your own business cards should be maintained in pristine condition – you too must consider your Face!

Case Study – Getting Business Cards Fatally Wrong

A top-flight Asian business school flew to Britain to investigate setting up a strategic partnership with one of UK's oldest and a Global Top Fifty business establishment.

The delegation was shown into the comfortable oak lined and leather upholstered lounge in one of the august buildings which made up the School. The Dean however was not there to meet his guests. But when he eventually arrived and business cards were exchanged, he relaxed back in his comfortable chair and asked gently what his visitors actually expected to be able to do for his famous establishment. Whilst he said this he folded the senior visitor's card carefully thrice and then pushed it underneath the glass top to the coffee table in front of him.

The visitors squirmed at the disrespect shown to their leader, politely drank their coffee, plead a pressing engagement and departed taking their offer of significant foreign currency injection with them.

And when you order your cards, order lots. Everyone that you meet will have a card that they wish to give you. A good planning figure is 500 for a week's visit.

When you return from a very busy and tiring business trip to China, you may want to establish closer contact with potential working partners or new customers. These are real business-builders so here are a few tips on making a good use of cards you receive:

1.   Bring a business card holder

2.   Immediately after the meeting:

   a)   Put all cards in the order of date and location received.
   b)   File in the order of ranking, if they are from a same company/organization/group.
   c)   Write down your impression of the person, his/her physical appearance, their attitude toward yourself/ your business/company, etc.
   d)   Note down any conversation you have had with the bearer, indicating whether his/her job title as shown on the card is relevant to what he/she does daily and if that's directly linking to what you are doing.

The Mayor of Weihai City Mme Hui Zhang and Weihai Link Treasurer Mr Tim Howard exchanging business cards – April 2012.

The use of both hands also extends to paying for things.

Case Study – The Honourable Barber

Shortly before Britain returned the colony of Hong Kong to the Peoples' Republic of China, the elderly Chinese barber, Mr Lee, on the garrison island of Stonecutters' presented one of his customers with an interesting certificate. This customer ran the Chinese Naval Division for the Royal Navy and so had a great deal to do with the local Chinese sailors and their supporting staff. Out of sheer habit, he had always paid for his haircuts using both hands as he normally did when dealing with the Chinese. Such was the esteem that this act gave to him that he created a bit of a reputation for honesty and straight dealing.

The reason for using both hands to pass and receive cards and cash is based on showing trust as these vignettes show.

Chinese courtesies

In conversation, difficult issues are avoided and particularly with senior men, tact is all. They expect to be able to glide through every encounter unchallenged.

Queues as we are brought up to respect in the UK just do not exist in China. If you are with Chinese friends, they will make sure that you get attention very fast but if you know no-one around then you are on your own and no-one will think the less of you if you jostle with the best of them.

Chinese versions of websites

If you don't have a website, you don't exist. This is true, not just for the Western world but even more so for China where the number of internet users now exceeds 400 million. This makes China the world's largest online community.

If you want to offer your services or products to Chinese markets, having a Chinese version of your company website is essential. It will enable you to communicate with targeted customers and, as crucially, it demonstrates your commitment to the China market.

Translating your site involves more than just translating text into Chinese as the Chinese version of website should be designed to be visually and culturally suitable for Chinese readers. It needs an entirely new design, from images and colour choice to layout and navigation.

In practice this means:

1. A high standard translation for its contents.
2. Photos and images suited to Chinese culture.
3. Layout and navigation are often seen as very full and busy with new windows popping up all the time.
4. Text often grouped by boxes.

A well structured, navigable and informative website always helps.

Other homework prior to embarking on trade with China

1. Do your market research about your services or products, potential business partners and competitors in much greater depth than you would in the West. Do make use of the many free Chinese government resources and seek professional help from people who have local business knowledge. It is always important to use multiple resources and cross check the outcome.

2. For your initial visit, your marketing material should be in English and translated into Chinese to make the best impact. It should include what you have to offer, why you are credible and reputable, how people should contact you with reference to your website for further information. It should be bold and colourful. The layout and appearance of English and Chinese marketing brochure can be very different, although the contents are the same.

3. Remember China is a very big country. You need to ensure your China business strategy includes expanding to new areas, and how to manage regional complexity. A business local to a coastal city will not be the same as inland and a branch in south China will not be the same in the north.

4. Add extra budget for activities to build and develop valuable relationships and networks.

5. Be patient and persistent in preparation and be ready to face the challenges ahead.

Don't forget your normal business instincts.

Gift giving

Lavish gift giving is an important part of Chinese culture, because it is a way of express gratitude, friendship, and hospitality. Nowadays, it is still considered necessary to have this customary reciprocity to build friendship. However, official policy in Chinese business restrains it, because of bribery. Therefore, in the business world, it is important to be sensitive when choosing to give a gift in a business context.

A company gift to a company is usually presented by the highest ranking person of both parties, with a formal photos session to record the event. You may need to explain where the gift is from, or the meaning of the gift to the receiver while presenting. The gift can be symbolic, but the wrapping must be appropriate. It is a show, so ensure you check when will be the best time or you may miss the opportunity or cause embarrassment.

For an individual gift, be prepared for the Chinese to decline the offer initially, so do offer again, and they may decline again, only accepting on the third time. This varies upon the circumstance, the region of China and the person's upbringing. Remember this is a ceremony, so do not turn around and offer it to next person immediately after being declined for the first time.

Here are a few tips on the etiquette of gift giving:

1. A gesture of personal friendship or thanks to a person should be private.
2. Often, gifts are not opened in the presence of the giver.
3. In the presence of other people, never present gifts of different values to different people.
4. If you did not bring any gifts, there is always next time, so don't panic.
5. Appreciated gifts include art, crafts, food and drink from your country, city or town – if you are Scots, whisky is always acceptable and if you are French, a good wine will be a winner.
6. Gifts wrapped in red or gold coloured paper are considered lucky. Never yellow, black or white, because they are associated with death. It is also best to have the wrapping done in China.
7. When you signing a greetings card, do not use red ink, which symbolizes the severing ties or being financially in the red.

Cheltenham Mayor Barbara Driver presenting a gift to Weihai Mayor Hui Zhang – April 2012

Cheltenham Borough Council Chief Executive Andrew North receiving a gift from Weihai Mayor Hui Zhang – April 2012

Meetings

Appointments should be made in advance, either yourself or through a 'guanxi' and always set to an agenda.

Do provide extra information about your company, yourself and who else would accompany you, especially if you are going to discuss technical issues.

In addition explain what you want to accomplish before the meeting so that the other side will be obliged to do the same. Extra efforts should be made to meet the 'right' person, even if you have to rearrange the time.

It is important to discuss the agenda with your interpreter prior to a meeting so that he or she knows just what you want (see separate section about interpreters).

Do avoid making appointments near Chinese New Year or other national holidays when you will experience great difficulty booking flights and when most people will not be available.

Greeting is a formal affair and often you are welcomed by a group of people waiting at the main entrance of the building, led by a senior person in the organisation. The building is often decorated with a big banner welcoming you.

It is really important that you arrive on time. Handshakes are the most common form of greeting with foreigners. When a female is present, wait for her to offer her hand first, or a nod with slight bow might be more appropriate.

You will be escorted to a meeting room, when it is assumed that the first person that enters the room is the head of the group in China. Further greeting and introduction, and business card exchange will take place.

Address a Chinese person by their surname and job/honorific title, e.g. Chairman Zhang, Managing Director Wang or Chief Li. Do not move to a first-name basis, even if they suggest this.

A meeting at Wego Group in Weihai April 2012
(Name plaques are in both English and Chinese, with pink card being most common)

Your presentation should be detailed and factual, focusing on all the long-term benefits and all the positives. If it's in English, you need to ensure you have graphic charts, and good visual images, plus an excellent interpreter who knows your content! Hand-out material should be available in both English and Chinese, using simplified characters.

The senior person present will tend to dominate the meeting for lengthy periods of time with other participants perhaps being offered an opportunity to contribute a section, but most people will just be present to listen. Your questions should be addressed to the senior person, even if it may be re-directed to some other attendee.

Meetings require patience, mobile phones may ring frequently, people may smoke without asking permission and discussions may not follow the agenda closely. Regardless, never ask the Chinese to turn off their mobile phones as this causes you both to lose Face. Remember always talk and face to your host directly, not to the interpreter, when the host is present.

A promotion meeting at Harbin institute of Technology of Weihai April 2012

One legacy from Imperial and Communist days has been the proclivity of the Chinese for detailed planning and record keeping. Prior to any meeting or venture, enormous administrative preparations will be made and discussed in far greater depth and across far more levels than you are used to – it will be very much a group affair. When it comes to the event, copious notes will be taken. These will then be digested in a similar manner afterwards and then brought into play during subsequent meetings. Woe betide the badly briefed, rushed or forgetful westerner who has not spent enough time in preparation. The Chinese will demand detailed responses there and then and be mightily unimpressed by promises to investigate and report back separately. You will be dealing not just with one or two people but probably dozens of their colleagues who have all had their input and made their demands for action or information.

Meals

Eating is a very serious matter in China and there are a number of protocols in behaviour to be aware of. They remain an intrinsic part of doing business in China and are also invaluable opportunity to build rapport with the Chinese side. Even more importantly, very senior figures may attend banquets whom you may not previously have had the opportunity to meet, and they can give an indication of how matters are progressing. They can also be invaluable contacts to make and maintain for your future business. Meals normally begin very promptly and end just as swiftly. The host will expect the guests to begin to leave once the last course has been eaten.

When you invite your guests to the UK on business, you don't have to provide lavish banquets, but it is important to be served at a sit down meal. Finger food or snacks in your office is not acceptable, even if it is only for a business lunch. This is a way of acknowledging the status of your visitors and making them feel welcome.

Case study – Inviting a friend for tea in UK

Alan met Mr Wang in China through work and they got on very well, Alan being invited to Wang's for dinner a number of times. Mr Wang was then on a business trip in London and Alan invited him to his house. Mr Wang brought a present from his home-town for Alan. Alan infused some nice tea and they talked. Time flew by and it was nearly lunchtime. Alan asked Mr Wang if he wanted some lunch. Mr Wang said no. They drank more tea and talked, then said goodbye.

Afterthoughts

Alan: was very happy seeing his friend again and thought they had a good time together renewing their friendship.

Mr Wang: he felt just the opposite, feeling Alan was cold and unwelcoming. Maybe he did not like him any more or had he done something wrong, he wondered?

In China, if you are inviting a friend to your home, especially if he or she has travelled a long way, a nice meal is a standard way to welcome them. For the guest, a gift is a standard courtesy in recognition of their friendship. Mr Wang said 'no' to lunch out of politeness. Even though he was very hungry, Alan should have offered again, possibly a third, even a fourth time, and insisted. This misunderstanding could end their friendship.

Case study – On being invited to a friend's house for dinner in China

Helen and Lee were invited to the house of a Chinese friend, Li, for dinner. They bought a very big bunch of flowers, including some white and yellow chrysanthemums as present.

Li and his wife Mei took the flowers and looked bit shocked but thanked them for their gift. They then started bringing in delicious looking dinner dishes, 'starters', 'main course', and when they thought it was time for 'desserts', only then did Helen and Lee realise that dinner was going to be a ten-course meal!

Afterthought

Helen and Lee: had a lovely evening, loving the generous Chinese hospitality but wished they hadn't had so much of the first and second courses and so missed the opportunity to try all the different home-cooked dishes as they were too full to even try.

Li and Mei: white and yellow chrysanthemums are usual for funerals in China, as Helen and Lee should have known. As a result they thought Helen and Lee only liked the first two courses of the meal, and assumed that there was something wrong with the rest.

Colours are a huge part of Chinese culture and so be careful to ask when unsure about colours to use or give – a florist would have helped them choose had they asked.

Formal banquets

Everything about a formal banquet is prearranged down to each minute detail, especially if it is for an official visit. Seating plans, name cards, who is to give a speech and when, timings for photos, menus set to a budget and what kind of entertainment, etc. It is also very important to have your own interpreter if it is an official visit.

At a formal banquet, if you are head of your group, be prepared to give a short, friendly speech in response to the host's speech.

Seating plans

In social business event settings such as banquets or dinners, round tables or long table(s) may be used and the seating rules will differ.

The round table

The principal host of a Chinese banquet is seated facing the door to the room or the stage if the meeting is taking place in an entertainment venue. The principal guest will be seated at the left of the principal host. If an interpreter is needed, he/she will be seated to the principal guest's immediate right or behind (often not having a meal). Generally, the seat is ranked by distance from the main host from high to low. Spouses of foreign guests are formally invited in China now. In such situations, the interpreter would generally then sit to the spouse's immediate right. Every effort is made to show the highest-ranking guests the respect they deserve within the Chinese culture.

A welcome banquet hosted by the Mayor of Weihai with traditional Chinese entertainments – April 2012

The second-ranking host will generally sit directly opposite the principal host, and with the second-ranking guest on the same table. If it is a big party, the Chinese will try to then use a second, third, forth table and repeat the ranking seating arrangement.

A long rectangular-shaped room/table

For a very formal meeting, the principal host and guest are always seated at the head of table with both side's interpreters seated behind. Other hosts and guests seated at each side, in the order of seniority, higher-ranking individuals closer to the head. Not all present at the meeting may be involved in the discussions.

The Official Cheltenham-Weihai Mayors' meeting April 2012

Toasts

If all has gone really well, then there is likely to be a great number of toasts drunk and this calls for strategy and a strong head. The Chinese do not as a rule regard drinking on its own as a social pastime as is the case in the West but rather they enjoy drinking with food. Hospitable beyond measure, your glass will miraculously top up although the marathon heady toasting sessions are increasingly confined to less developed cities. So much so that, in the large coastal cities, they are almost a thing of the past. However, further inland the Chinese will have their own answer to the legendary drinker Lau Ling with them and it is important to plan for this. He will have only one aim and that is to prove that he can outdrink the Westerners. He will probably not be involved in detailed negotiations the next day, but you will.

Weihai Deputy Mayor Zhiying Tian hosting author YingShi Helsby – April 2012

What to wear?

Business attire is conservative and unpretentious. Dark-coloured business suits are preferred for men and women and women's dresses or tops should be conservative with a high neckline. Attitudes in China are conservative as was found on a recent trip to China when a visiting businesswoman's slightly décolleté top – completely in tune with British fashion – did raise a concern with her Chinese hostess. It is best to remember that in this business environment you are dressing to someone else's code and not to your own.

Who pays for the meal?

Graciously receive the hospitality when invited to a formal banquet as most likely the Chinese side is hosting and paying. In some parts of China, especially if you are not in coastal cities, although senior local officials host the welcoming party, you might be expected to contribute some or all of the cost of the banquet. Check this out beforehand and be prepared. Do remember to pay the compliment back when they come to visit you!

Eating together is an important bonding session for business partners and colleagues for informal social or business meals in China. The matter of who pays the meal and how is straightforward. It is not quite like having a drink in a pub in England. You pay this time, your friend will pay next, never split the bill. 'Fight' to pay the bill, even if there is a 'prearrangement' in place. Beware, the income of your Chinese colleagues and friends may be much lower than yours. If they seem a bit hesitant to eat out, it might be helpful to choose more reasonably priced places, the food will be just as good, but the facilities might be basic. On ordering food, you might notice that Chinese people always 'waste' far too much food. Most of time they order a range dishes consisting of different kinds of meat, sea food, vegetables for everybody to share, all accompanied with far too much alcohol. It is the Chinese way. If you order just your own food and are keen not to share, you might be seen as unfriendly. If you are on a special diet, that would be a different matter.

Interpreters

If an interpreter is paid to represent your opponent, naturally his/her loyalty will not be with you. It is imperative that you bring or pay for your own interpreter at important business negotiations. The extra cost will worth every penny for your business.

He/she will not just be conveying conversation between two parties. They will represent your best interests, act as your eyes, and ears, and explain everything important to you. He/she may also give you their understanding of the situation, 'translating' body language, pointing out who is the real key person for your business. They will help you by covering remarks you made which might offend the

Chinese by not translating it, even act as your spy, telling you Chinese people's internal dialogues to give you vital information you may need to seal a deal.

A good interpreter should understand both cultures really well. Beware some interpreters in China might be fluent in English, but might never have been to the West. Their understanding of Western culture can therefore be superficial.

Some tips for you to work well with interpreters:

1. Brief the interpreters in advance about your company, yourself, what you are trying to achieve.
2. Give him or her time to become familiar with any or industry-specific jargon. It is wise to create a technical vocabulary list unless he or she works or has worked in the same industry.
3. Agree on a general strategy prior a meeting on whether you want every sentence translated or merely a summary.
4. Force yourself to speak slowly, using short, simple, clear sentences. Avoid analogies, slang or culturally referenced words.
5. Remember that you are the boss and do not let the interpreter speak for you, and never let him/her negotiate a deal for you. You have to be in control of all of the conversation.

Official Cheltenham-Weihai Mayors' meeting – April 2012

Case study – The Interpreter

Andy is a purchasing manager in an international company. On a buying trip to China, he asks a simple question on a key component for his product – 'How long is the lead time?' The Chinese side talk amongst themselves for a while then the interpreter translates this as '15 days'.

If the interpreter had been paid by Andy's company, he or she would have explained that the sales person really wanted this order because of his sales targets, so insisted on offering 15 days for delivery even though he knew this would not be possible. The factory production team had been experiencing problems with their raw material supplier for some time so 15 days was just not achievable nor could it be guaranteed in the future either. The General Manager already knew this product could not be delivered without changing the supplier, but this information could not be released to Andy just yet...

The factory-supplied interpreter just said '15 days'. Can you imagine what Andy might say to his own production team later when their key component is not delivered on time?

Who matters?

This can be very hard in China. A result of Face – 面子 (miànzi) – is that no one and particularly not those in any position of authority will ever put themselves willingly in a position where they might be shown up in any way. So junior representatives will normally conduct all initial discussions or meetings and report back to their superiors for further instructions and decisions. Therefore, do not be frustrated or irritated if it seems to take an age to speak to the real movers and shakers. The Chinese side is merely marshalling their resources and making sure that no one gets embarrassed by inadvertent ineptitude. By the same token you need to check exactly who it is that you are dealing with to make sure that you get to deal with the decision-maker. Remember it's not London's Canary Wharf or Edinburgh's New Town and it will pay you to persevere – it is just how business is done in China or as they say 这是中国！(Zhè shì Zhōngguó) – that's China! The observant guest can also learn much about relative statuses by watching who sits where during meals.

Case Study – Succeeding in China

Meetings don't always turn out the way you plan. Having been asked by one of his Chinese associate to pay a courtesy call on the Chairman of the local Council for Small and Medium Enterprises whilst in Beijing, the author duly made his way to Mr Sheng's office in the north-west of the capital. This was clearly going to be an invaluable long-term contact he thought as pleasantries and tea were shared in the Council office festooned with photographs of senior government officials during their own visits, but when? As the pair chatted and the Chairman's ex-PLA secretary and the author exchanged banter about their military pasts, two younger men joined them and sat down. One clearly spoke no English but was bursting with nervous energy, the other, a much larger and more considered man turned out to have taken two degrees in UK.

As the meeting drew to a close the author thanked the Chairman for his time and hospitality and promised to pass the details of his Council on to his own Chamber of Commerce, and then found himself whisked away by the two latecomers. As they drove off, the trio commented on the good work being done to build business from the bottom up in the new commercial China by the Council and the opportunities which this would in turn provide for foreign investors.

Then, matters began to clarify themselves. The party arrived in at the offices of a PR company in the erstwhile Asian Student Games village. There were two further appointments arranged for the visitor. The first was to the PR organization who wished to grow their business internationally. Television shows were one focus and the other was their modelling agency which was looking at involvement in China's ambitions in the Formula One motor racing sector. Their reasoning was that although they had an established and reputable school for models with a large number of beautiful ladies on their books and whilst the fashion trade in the capital provided good business for all, if they could only join forces with the racing organizers in China, the marketing mix of unique location, western racing cars, low cost base and elegant Chinese models would be unbeatable. They did, however, recognize one serious shortcoming. Their ladies were fantastically photogenic but had no idea as to how to conduct themselves in the international sporting arena. Could their foreign visitor possibly assist – and the answer from the cross-cultural traveller was happily for all concerned, 'yes!' The contact was in no way fortuitous, a lot of telephone calls had been made well before the visit to the Council of Small and Medium Enterprises and only needed a little flexibility from the visitor not to become phased as people came and went during his call on a Government official.

Closure

Closure is perhaps the most difficult and elusive issue of all in doing business in China for Westerners. This is because in their Behaviours and Communications the Chinese default to harmony in all matters. Therefore they will not be trying to 'string you along' by being non-committal, they just do not want to disappoint you and create disharmony by rejecting your proposal. In China, no news is most definitely not good news. When they wish something to happen they will ramp up the pace of events to an often-staggering level. At this point it is often a useful tactic to keep this particular part of the game to a speed with which you are comfortable and at which you can deliver. If you really have a product or a solution of relevance and you have made sure your offering is understood, then all should you are in for a chance.

Follow-up

As we have seen, the Chinese are wish to see real commitment from potential and existing business partners and so the importance of methodically following up on all the important business contacts you make it critical to your business success; if you fail to show this commitment to the China Market then you should not expect too much – it is all up to you.

7

RISK MANAGEMENT IN CHINA

China has become a dominant force in the global economy with many foreign investors looking at mainland China in an attempt to find better economic solutions. Opening a China operation is a complex business. Without conducting a thorough risk assessment and consulting business advisers with local knowledge, companies may face unfamiliar perils. Get business strategy wrong and you may face a painful and expensive experience.

Legal framework

In China, the legal system more closely resembles Civil Law systems than Common Law systems. There are two regulations which provide the primary framework regulating foreigner direct investments in China.

Firstly, the Chinese *Catalog for the Guidance of Foreign Investment Industries* restricts foreign investment to specified sectors (promulgated in 2006，revised in 2007 and 2011). It is intended as a guide for foreign investors. It assigns industry sectors to one of three categories: "encouraged," "restricted," and "prohibited". Industries that do not fall within "encouraged", "restricted" or "prohibited" are generally deemed "permitted" industries.

Changes in the new version (2011 edition) include:

1. Manufacturing industries. Foreign investment is encouraged in strategic industries such as energy-saving and environmental protection, new-generation information technology, biology, high-end equipment manufacturing, new energy, new materials and new energy vehicles.

2. Service industries. Foreign investment is encouraged in "modern" service industries. Nine service industry have been added to the encouraged category in the new catalogue, including motor vehicle charging stations, venture capital enterprises, intellectual property services, marine oil pollution clean-up technical services, vocational skills training, etc. Meanwhile, foreign-invested medical institutions and finance lease companies have been moved from the restricted to the permitted category.

3. Commercial and healthcare industries. Commercial entities relating to franchising, entrusted operation and business management have been removed from the restricted category. The wholesale, retail and distribution of pharmaceuticals has been reclassified from the restricted to the permitted category. Also, foreign investment in medical care institutions is now classified as permitted as opposed to restricted.

4. Media and publication industries. Under the 2011 Catalogue, foreign investors are no longer prohibited from investing in the main distribution and import of books, newspapers and magazines, the import of audio and visual products and electronic publications or music-related Internet culture business. However, foreign investment in the publication of books, newspapers and magazines, the publication and production audio and visual products and electronic publications and operation of news websites, provision of audio and video programs on network, operation of business premises for Internet-access services and Internet culture business (excluding music) remain prohibited.

The second important set of rules is the *Provisions on Mergers and Acquisition of a Domestic Enterprise by Foreign Investors*. You should check the latest version of the regulations to make sure if the investment plan is legally workable.

Business entities
The main investment vehicles in China are:

- Representative office (RO)
- Wholly foreign-owned enterprise (WFOE)
- Equity joint venture (EJV)
- Cooperative joint venture (CJV)
- Foreign invested commercial enterprise (FICE)

Establishing and registering a new company in China
Some foreign businessman and entrepreneurs might be frustrated by the unfamiliar environment in which they are starting a new business. For example the bureaucracy involved in the seemingly process of just registering a business may have a high cost which does not contribute to productive business investment. Couple this with the lengthy time it takes to complete the process and the language barriers and the outside investor may be tempted to try to follow the locals who can often use 'short cuts'. However, this creates high risks for the company's future.

Case study – Pizza restaurant chain

The Kro's Nest 乌巢披萨店 *(Wū cháo pīsà diàn), Courtyard 4, Gongti Beilu, Chaoyang District, Beijing, China*

The Kro's Nest boasted serving the best pizza in Beijing. There was an ownership dispute. Olaf Kristoffer Bauer aka Kro 庄小龙 *(Zhuāng Xiǎolóng), a young American entrepreneur, claimed he started a business partnership with Yuan Jie* 袁捷 *(Yuán jié), building up the The Kro's Nest together. He said they were both eager for the pizza restaurant's full operation by the quickest possible route. Yuan handled the company's legal issues, because he was local Chinese; Kro focused on the restaurant's operation and brand building, because that was his strength. A few years on, the Kro's Nest become a success story: Kro starred in CCTV (China Central Television) cooking shows, and appeared* in a FHM celebrity photo shoot, on multiple international magazine covers and was treated like a celebrity by Chinese gossip magazines. He was proclaimed a restaurant prodigy by Beijing's English language press. Naturally customers came pouring in.

However, today Kro is no longer working at Kro's Nest. Kro's former partner, Yuan Jie and his wife – a former employee turned accountant, Zhang Yan 张妍 (Zhāng Yán) – still are. Yuan maintains he started the company and hired Kro to build the brand.

This was a well-publicised case in China. There was some evidence of an earnest effort to turn the Kro's Nest into a legal entity at an early stage. However, that was not taken to completion.

Important Lessons:

1. Oral business agreement on business decision is very important in China, but it should always be followed with formal papers or/and legal documentation.

2. Ensure you are fully involved with your partner(s) and seek local professional help on legal issues

3. Make the ownership and structure of your company clear to all parties involved.

Intellectual property protection

The Chinese traditionally believe that ideas and knowledge cannot be owned, especially if people can make a living from it. If you have the ability and are able to learn it, it belongs to you. Without legal means to protect your invention, you could find yourself out of profits, out of competition, and out of existence very quickly.

China is the world's second-largest market for computer hardware sales. However, it is only the eighth-largest for software sales. In joining the World Trade Organization in 2001, China promised to do away with intellectual property theft. The Chinese attitude to intellectual property rights will change over time due to rising average GDP per person and international pressures. But until that time comes, you still have the challenge of protecting your intellectual assets.

With its booming economy, huge manufacturing base, relatively well educated work force and cheap labour costs, all coupled with an enormous supply of natural resources, it's no surprise many businesses around the world are sourcing their product in China. Among the critical risks are mergers and acquisitions, production interruption, retention of employees and, most importantly, intellectual property protection issues.

It is vital for you to insist on confidentiality and protection of all information about your company, and product by signing a Non-Disclosure Agreement. Make sure the sourcing company understands prudence. Keep your product specifications, technical written and drawings and other documents in secure locations. Keep staff motivated and carry out regular inspections backed-up with good reporting systems. It is unlikely you will remain the only client for all time, even if you are maintaining a good relationship for now. Fair pricing, long-term contracts and mutual benefit will do much to ensure the long life of any partnerships.

Case study

A well known international motorbike company has licensed components direct from a factory in China for many years very successfully. Their competitor approached the same factory trying to source similar components and offered much more attractive deals to the factory. A court case was brought that it had infringed the component's patents. While this was going on the motorbike company was not able to trade and was suffering huge financial losses. Luckily for this company, the court ruled in their favour and they are back to business.

Lessons Learned:

1. The factory owner in China did sign an NDA but was not fully aware of the consequences of breeching it. Intellectual property does not only include patented technology, trademarks, copyrights, but also business plans and who has access to it at what level.

2. *Information security processes (including IT security), incident-management procedures, business continuity plans, protection policies and procedures should be reviewed regularly.*

3. *All staff working in this area should be trained in Intellectual Property protection.*

Product safety and liability

Chinese has a tendency towards investing heavily in a new client until they receive a contract. They are more than willing to give you everything you want, including cost breakdowns, excellent product samples (often far better quality and packaging then the usual product itself), even some secrets of technical product details. The first few deliveries can be heavily subsidized until they received payment. However, once you became a regular customer, the quality of goods you receive may deteriorate.

There are many example of items made in China recalled after the discovery of safety issues, such as paint containing excessive levels of lead. Such issues pose a significant risk to your company's brand and reputation. Among the steps companies can take to reduce the likelihood and severity of major product-safety events from their China operations are to instil a quality control and audit supply-chain production system, monitoring products regularly, establish a management system for product safety and liability, implement product-recall plans and to have a compliant products liability insurance.

8

NEGOTIATING – CHINESE-STYLE

Business negotiation

As a westerner, for most business negotiations, you are most likely to focus on tasks, attempting to complete them in a fixed time in specific terms and conditions, in other words "results-oriented". For most Chinese people, they are more focusing on harmony and flexibility, in another words "relationship-oriented".

A negotiation will only take place if your prospective Chinese business partner feels your relationships have developed to the stage at which they feel comfortable to do business with you. Often it is after you have gone through numerous banquets, meetings and gifts exchanges that you 'get to know each other'. Once negotiations are started, it can be painfully slow. Chinese are non-confrontational, they often say, 'well, we will be thinking about it', 'let's see' instead of a direct 'no'. Similarly, you will hear a 'yes' response to almost everything, so be aware these 'yes's' may means 'yes, I'm listening' or 'yes, I hear what you say', not what you've expected, a positive conclusion. If you are unsure of an answer, just reword your question and ask again.

Chinese often hesitate to provide full information at the beginning, sometimes it is like squeezing toothpaste. Using mutual contacts usually helps, until trust and credibility are establishing with your Chinese counterpart. Be prepared for tough negotiations. Adhere to your principles and objectives. If problems develop, you should be firm about your limits and your willingness to work with your counterparts to find a mutually agreeable solution. A decision may take a long time, as they often go through lengthy internal review and consideration. Under no circumstances should you lose your temper or you will lose Face and irrevocably damage your relationship.

The Chinese have varying business styles in different regions, as if they are different countries. People in coastal cities are more likely be adamant about having things their own way and you should be firm about you position in a negotiation.

Most formal deals should have a firm shape before you reach the negotiation room, to discuss the details. Be patient, make sure your interpretation of the contract is correct and let the Chinese know you are prepared to walk away rather than agree to a bad deal. The Chinese usually conclude deals over a meal and this entertaining is a critical part of Chinese business culture.

There is a fundamental difference in perception and attitude on finalising the contract agreement. For the Chinese, formalisation of a contract does not imply that it is final and fixed. It is an agreement of a relationship, powers of both parties are balanced, and both parties do really understand each other. It shows that there is now a platform for further trading and mutual exchange of favours and a start for the next chapter in the relationship, not an end result.

Chinese negotiators are master of a variety of different tactics. *The Art of War* summarised thirty-six strategies to deflect opponents. It was, as we have seen, written over two thousand five hundred years ago (please see the Art of War section in Chapter 2 for more details), but all tactics described are still very Today. Most top military personal, politicians, business people study it. Do read it if you have not done so already.

Millennia of practice

Whilst you can argue that all people have been trading ever since prehistoric days, what makes China singular is the simple fact that the Chinese identify with the continuity of their culture over thousands of years in a way that those with European roots do not. As a direct result of this, the Chinese trading and negotiating culture has developed hand in hand with the more general culture. What this means to us as foreigners in China is that we are faced with highly skilled, ruthless and instinctive negotiators who regard this aspect of business as a very serious and separate skill. They do not believe in win-win but will still seek to restore harmonious relations afterwards. You will need patience, time and awareness of what may lie ahead as you approach the negotiating table.

Author YingShi Helsby at the 2013 China Import and Export Fair (Canton Fair)

British Buyer Nic Stone at the 2013 China Import and Export Fair (Canton Fair)

The Chinese view

Harmony will always be the aim at the end of any set of negotiations in the People's Republic of China, whatever has passed before. That is worth remembering as you work towards agreement with an adversary more skilled in the tactics of the street market world in which win-win has little place. In many ways the Chinese see themselves on the stage during negotiations and allow themselves to act in ways they would not allow themselves to do in normal business or social intercourse. In this way they can shout, appear to lose their temper, use false authority, or be cold and attacking around the table. You need to be mentally prepared for very different discussions.

Chinese team tactics

As group – oriented race, the Chinese will negotiate as a team. You will notice that different people come and go. This is partly to unsettle you and partly to make sure that the senior negotiators are not presented with a *fait accompli* and are not exposed to any danger of embarrassing themselves in public.

Before opening the negotiation proper, it is always best to be prepared to talk around the issue until everyone present is settled and ready. At the start you may well find that the opening positions may appear unrealistic – they probably are so that both sides can make concessions without losing Face and feel that they are winning.

Suspicion of foreigners may lead to adversarial exchanges and if you can deploy all your patience and forbearance to deflect and defuse this tactic, then you will gain Face with the Chinese as an experienced and worthy opponent.

One of the most exasperating tactics is for questions to be asked time and time again. Partly this is for verification, partly for ensuring meeting notes are correct, partly to glean as much as possible about western business skills and there will still be concealed agenda items. You can of course counter this yourself by going back repeatedly to any issue you choose.

A development of this is for previously agreed heads to be revisited. This is to put you off your negotiating stride and force concessions.

All Asians know well the power of silence as a negotiating tool with Westerners who may the feel the compulsive need to fill the void by an unwitting concession – be warned and try using silence at home and see the result.

As with all things in Asia, Face is ever present and you can show your own negotiating abilities by leaving graceful exit routes for the Chinese side as you work towards closure. It is also well worth your while letting them know that you will accept failure to agree as an acceptable result or that they are not the only option being explored.

The received wisdom is that foreigners should never lose their tempers when in Asia. This is true. However, there are occasions when the Chinese will not think that you are being serious unless you do show anger – but choose you moments very carefully!

As the time draws near for you and your team to leave China, expect delaying tactics to load you with pressure to agree so as to get to the airport on time. If matters stall, then accept that and make moves to return to your hotel and 'enjoy' a break. An emissary may well then appear seeking some concession to enable dialogue to be reopened. When all is agreed, happily move on to the restaurant and or karaoke. You are now showing acceptance of Chinese culture and respect for China.

Negotiation rhythm

As negotiations open with the Chinese you will probably find them taking a very moderate and moralistic stance and this may even take the form of a lecture on the inequalities of history and how the West should now act as a benefactor of China (regardless of whatever shadowy forces may have been at work in such instances as McDonald's being eased out of their prime site in Beijing shortly after opening, for example). Merely smile and hear all.

Once serious negotiations get going you will find the pace hotting up as Chinese voices begin to get raised and exchanges verge on the confrontational. There will doubtless be some fairly tough talking on its way with frequent references to and use of status and power. As agreement gets closer and people's positions become clearer you will be aware that a lot of negotiation will have been going on behind the scenes and that this has been holding everything together.

With sighs of relief all round, agreement will be reached and harmony restored as you shake hands and prepare, hopefully for the celebratory banquet.

Conflict management

One can pre-empt much of the potential conflict in negotiation by being punctilious in showing respect to the other side whilst remaining firm in your manner. Respect should be accorded to age and status.

Another source of conflict is if the Chinese suspect that you have been too casual in your preparations and this they will take as an insult rather than regard as a shortcoming on your behalf.

If matters do deteriorate into a shouting match, do not respond in kind. There is every chance that the outbursts from the Chinese are a careful ploy designed to fluster you into making rash decisions. If, on the other hand, the Chinese side have lost control, such will be their embarrassment at their behaviour that you have an additional task in attempting to help them restore their Face.

Discretion

Things may be said or heard during negotiations, which are probably, best kept in the boardroom to avoid creating additional tensions. Certainly if the negotiations extend over a significant period of time with evenings spent in karaoke bars treat the events with caution and do not leave yourself vulnerable to having to make unwanted concessions to prevent rumours of indiscrete behaviour getting out. The karaoke is loved across Asia as one of the very rare opportunities in which the men can relax and open themselves up to a tremendous degree. Even if you believe that you cannot sing, do not worry because many of the other songsters cannot – just enjoy it for what it is, have a few pop songs in mind for when the microphone gets handed to you and literally sing a song to your opposite number, you will gain great Face too this way. Try not to enjoy the hospitality too much either since a lot of business deals are concluded in the karaoke and you need a clear head for the morning.

Patience

Negotiation is a serious business in China and you will need to deploy every ounce of patience that you have and more. One of the most useful tools that the Chinese use is to try the patience of those with whom they are dealing. The result that they are after will be a loss of 'cool' and embarrassing outbursts which will give them the upper hand. But do not be misled when they use controlled bursts of anger and insult to make points, you should never respond in kind. By remaining cool, calm and collected whatever the provocation you will gain enormous respect as a good negotiator.

In showing a broad understanding of and sympathy for the cultural drivers in China you will also gain esteem.

There is no need to shout or try to rush the opposite side although there is every value in letting them know that you do not necessarily regard them as the only possible partners.

Preparation and record keeping

Confucius imposed an orderliness on Chinese life and fifty years of Communist administration have done nothing to dilute this. You may be pretty satisfied, and with good reason, with the preparations and care that you have put into business meetings. However, until you have negotiated with the Chinese you are a mere beginner. The Chinese view is that there can never be enough effort put into the preparation for a meeting, and especially with Westerners. You will already have picked up that Face is involved here. To be found wanting in any way in meetings with Chinese or foreigners would result in an unacceptable loss of Face. You, in turn, will also be expected to prepare to the nth degree. If you do not then the Chinese will show no mercy as they apply their favoured 'win-lose' philosophy to negotiation. Records of statements or positions taken in previous meetings will be produced for your explanation or further negotiation but you can give Face to your Chinese counterparts by keeping records of the positions they have taken in previous meetings and referring back them in your own notes yourself – you will gather that we are fans of keeping workbooks in business and certainly they are in China. Things can move very fast in China even when the pace of negotiations seems agonizingly slow.

9

DEVELOPING BUSINESS IN CHINA

China today

Beginning in 1978 Deng Xiaoping led China to embark upon economic reform – changing China's centrally-planned form of 'state capitalism' to a 'socialist market economy'. In the brief time since 1978, China has once again emerged a significant economic power and the standard of living of the majority of Chinese citizens, is increasing exponentially.

China is a one-party state, with the ruling Communist Party of China (CPC) effectively unchallenged in its dominance of the political system. Parallel CPC structures in the government, bureaucracy and military mean that the CPC holds real power at every level. However, contrary to the image of a rigid, rusting communist regime, the CPC has transformed itself in the reform era (from 1978), in many respects proving flexible, pragmatic and competent. Old-style central planning has disappeared, but the state still strongly influences development of key sectors and retains interventionist tendencies. After ten years under the previous leadership, headed by President Hu Jintao and Premier Wen Jiabao, a scheduled transfer of power will put in place a 'fifth generation' of leaders under Xi Jinping take over many key CPC and state posts in 2012 and 2013.

China's extraordinary economic development has brought extremely impressive achievements, but also very serious problems associated with such high-speed, large-scale growth and transformation. These include rising inequality, environmental degradation, corruption and socio-economic dislocation. Significant discontent and social unrest are among the results, but do not currently threaten the regime. The political system is firmly established; while its flaws are serious and widely recognised, its legitimacy and resilience are based on more than just GDP growth and nationalism.

China is attempting to shift its growth model, from a 'growth at all costs' approach that clearly cannot continue indefinitely to a more sustainable model. Leaders know growth is over-reliant on (often state-led) investment and exports, and want the share of consumption in GDP growth to increase. However, such rebalancing faces considerable practical and political obstacles, as does the creation of a more efficient and sustainable financing model. Meanwhile, major constraints on the local private sector and foreign investors remain, as market liberalisation has slowed to a crawl. Foreign companies also face systemic challenges such as corruption, opaque and inconsistently enforced regulation and inadequate legal protection. China's foreign relations have grown increasingly tense, but remain basically stable.

The Hukou system

The Hukou 戶口 (Hùkǒu) household registration system was adopted in 1958. It was originally set up to control the population migrating from rural areas to cities in search of work and better living conditions. Under the Hukou, Chinese citizens' birth registration classifies them as either 'rural' or 'urban' citizens. He/she would be entitled to receive state education or certain types of work permits and other benefits. This essentially (like a passport system between countries) made it very hard to move legally around the country at will.

It is thought at least ten percent of the Chinese make up a 'floating population' of migrant workers and their families with no Hukou, especially so since the Family Planning (one-child) Policy was put in place in 1978. The number is estimated at between 100 to 200 million people, coming mostly from rural areas.

Reform of the Hukou continues and many Chinese think-tanks

and prominent citizens have called for its complete elimination. But millions of Chinese depend on the Hukou system to ensure their benefits in old age. This is one reason the Hukou is being phased out gradually over time.

Managing business and relations

Face 面子 (miànzi) is the heart of all Chinese interaction and especially in terms of courtesy. In any dealings with Chinese people it is critical to respect this and for Westerners it is best understood as if you were trading with people who see themselves through other peoples' eyes – it is much more complex than this but it's a reasonable starting point. Face is closely linked to lian 脸 (liǎn) which refers to the confidence of society in the integrity of one's moral character, honour or ego, the loss of which makes it impossible for him or her to function properly within the community. Mianzi in this context refers to the kind of prestige that is emphasized in a reputation achieved through getting on in life, through success and ostentation. Face is about a Chinese person's self respect and prestige and their standing in the group. It is similar in west where one has one's self-esteem and are sensitive about personal credibility and dignity. Shame is felt in the West but not in the slightest to the same degree as in Asia,

Westerners need to be aware that Face can be lost by:

- direct face-to-face challenge in public, especially by a junior by position or age
- insulting someone intentionally or unintentionally
- cultural insensitivity or pure ignorance
- losing control in public by displaying anger
- declining an invitation to a social or business function with no good reason
- refusing a request
- refusing a gift
- even being too independent
- being aggressive
- displaying grief in public.

If you cause a Chinese to lose Face, the act may be forgiven, but it will never be forgotten, either by the unfortunate recipient or by those who observed the event. They will go to great and occasionally ludicrous lengths to preserve Face.

Case study – lack of confidence, insincerity or humility?

Ling has just been relocated from China to work in her Chinese employer's Bristol branch office. Her English is excellent, although she is not yet culturally attuned to the British way of life.

She often says 'sorry my English is so poor…', although most people would compliment her on how good her English is.

Her colleagues and friends think she's either insincere or lacking confidence, although she thinks she's being humble.

From Mianzi the foreign businessman or woman – the 外商 (wàishāng) – must grasp guanxi 关系 (guānxi). In China, no person exists except in relation to others and relationships are a form of social capital, owned by people – this far predates the redoubtable Hofstede but allowed him to clarify societies globally. This concept encompasses the unique Chinese world view that captures relationships as grounded in trust, mutual obligation and shared experience. It is a survival strategy with each individual linking their fate to an inner circle of family, friends and trusted associates from their home town, school, university or college or work unit 单位 (dānwèi) where they have lived for many years. It is a mind set evolved from centuries of wealth alternating with widespread poverty and has become a cultural pattern that persists powerfully today. Like most developing economies and country, China still however exists in a low-trust environment.

Chinese people do not feel comfortable or knowledgeable about dealing with strangers although they can be the kindest, most considerate and polite people you will ever meet. In a public situation, they can be as rude, impolite and inconsiderate. They wonder, themselves, how people from the same culture can behave so differently.

Guanxi in action – Melville Petrie with China's visionary No 2 Person – Admiral Liu Huaqing – in 1984

How then do you build the trust with these people?

There are two level of trust. The first is the logical trust that emanates from the confidence one has in a person's accomplishments, skills and reliability. This in some ways is easy and is measurable. Your partner is likely judging your competence based on your position in your company.

The second level of trust comes from feelings of emotional closeness, rapport and empathy. This is much harder to define as different cultures do not always have the same values or assumptions. If you share a cultural background with your Chinese partner, you will invariably enjoy a common ground of values and norms and this can form the powerful basis of interpersonal understanding. Or if you share cultural interests such as Chinese painting, the sophisticated rituals and art forms will bring you together. Or, if you are both fans of the same football club, you will find common ground to share. It is all a matter of discovering how to bridge the cultural difference and that is not so far removed from finding a way to relate to all your people, be they blue-collar Manchester City supporters, white-collar golf enthusiasts or boardroom pigeon fanciers, it is up to you to find a way to connect.

The Chinese have an elaborate networking system called guanxi. This is a network of obligations between 'friends' within networks and can be graded according to the status of those involved, how long-lasting it may be or whether or not it can be useful beyond the immediate network.

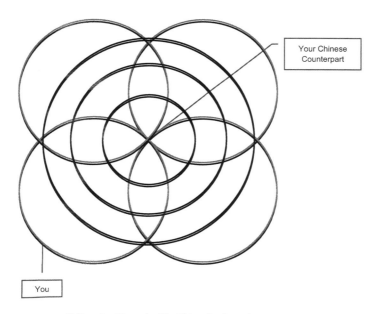

Your Chinese Counterpart

You

(Ming-Jer Chen, Inside China Business)

Establishing and building new guanxi often start from drinking, dining and entertainment and is what we consider as 'getting to know each other'. Chen Ming-Jer's map may help you to understand how to connect to the 'right person' and arrange a meeting via a network that you have in China. However a true guanxi does not stop there, it has to be mutually beneficial, with good will and possible long-term working relationships gradually building up more trust over years of working together, through the highs and lows of business and constant effort.

The contributions of Confucianism and Buddhism

From what we have already seen the cultural values considered important for successful business in the China market include interpersonal harmony first, then trust, followed by a sense of belonging, with guanxi a key determinant in successful business in China.

Important cultural values in the Chinese market

Do you need guanxi to do business in China? The answer is yes. It is critical in a business deal, helps better communication and frank negotiation. Also extra facilitation of everything you may need for business including local knowledge. However, a guanxi serves only in first introduction. There is no magic formula, it works because each party is carrying trust, benefit and the risk involved in the business.

Not only will the Chinese systematically follow-up with all new business contacts to explore the likelihood but also this is entirely accordance with the Confucian view of Li礼 (lǐ), polite and formal behaviour. Greeting cards will arrive punctually at annual festivals including Chinese New Year – so don't forget that yourself until it is clear that the new acquaintance will be of no value. The streak of pragmatism in the Chinese psyche is immensely strong. You too will need to be as methodical and as pragmatic as they if business is to build. Almost everything in China is relational and when you think about, so is much of the way things are done in Britain as well.

The key to getting things done in China is as much a matter as getting close to the people relevant to what you want to achieve as anything else. If you are trying to buy a number of new factory development sites, previous calls on local government officials or even better, the mayor, will enable you to move ahead. If you have just arrived in town and know nobody, little of any consequence is likely to be achieved. In terms of local government contacts, never ignore central government in Beijing. Without the right guanxi nothing will happen. To prove these contacts photographs with key figures can be invaluable and so once you begin to collect snapshots of yourself with influential figures, it pays to carry them with you to show your

Chinese business associates that you too can conform to the group oriented Chinese behaviour.

Case Study – Expansion Gone Wrong

A major French supermarket chain was growing very positively in Mainland China after a false start in Hong Kong. After 8 years it was in over 20 cities and employing over 20,000 people, it was spending over RMB 2 billion on goods and so could be considered a major player in the national retail sector. As individual prosperity increases in China the sector has been growing by 28% year on year. They had achieved much of its strategy through very deliberate and careful management of its relations with local government and by making great strides in helping the Chinese become more aware of environmental issues. This approach chose to focus solely on local and not Central Government. The Chinese view of the relationship between Beijing and the different provinces has changed little over the centuries since the Emperors ruled. They were far away in Beijing and there were many mountain ranges separately ruler and subjects. This in fact works both ways. Central Government sees its role as setting out policy and legislation and Local Governments' task to implement. If that implementation has to be adapted to resolve local circumstances and that presents no direct challenge or insult to Central Government, it is then content. When however the chain began to grow so fast that Chinese businesses began to complain to Central Government, the French paid the price of ignoring Beijing. They found themselves facing charges of operating against regulations and a government who had taken action to maintain competitiveness by merging the four major Chinese retailers and then splitting them into four strategic sub-units of hypermarkets, supermarkets, department stores and convenience stores. Further expansion for the foreigners then become more problematic. Immensely fast the pace of change may be, but China's behaviours remain deeply traditional. In Confucian terms, for Emperor, read Central Government and the matter becomes clear.

Establishing sound relationships in China is not impossible, it is just very different to the way it is achieved in UK and in the length of time it takes. This is a result of the nation being such a populous and literate nation and because it occupies such a huge and varied landmass and has great boundary sensitivities. Its long recorded history and written culture have imbued its people with a deep sense of nationhood, which borders on a sense of racial superiority. They have recently grasped western monetarist socialism and at the same time have neither sought nor been able to cast off Confucian thinking. As a people they are very family-centric and do not easily open themselves up to outsiders of whatever nature, Chinese or foreign.

Chinese personal relations

Chinese see themselves at the centre of the inner circle in the close company of family, friends and a few trusted associates. These 'friends' may be from the same place in which they grew up or studied with or served with in the PLA – whatever the link, the bond will be very strong indeed. This guanxi will facilitate all sorts of solutions be they in answer to personal or business issues. Around this, the next circle is populated by a fairly finite number of individuals who are either known well, are trusted to some extent or who belong to the inner circle of relatively close associates and with whom business or social intercourse can happily take place. Strangers of whatever ilk occupy the outer circle and with whom little contact is either required or even demanded. In this last context, it is absolutely acceptable, for example, for the head of an academic institute to get into the same lift as one of his staff in the morning without any acknowledgement, get into his or her car and drive off to work leaving her or his compatriot to find their own way to college. There they will have a frank and free professional relationship without any of the residual rancour that their peers in Europe or the US might feel. There would be free movement from the outer circle to the middle and it is this access that foreigners must aspire to and work towards if they wish to succeed in China.

Time, patience and openness are the three requirements for access to this vital business zone. The Chinese have got to have time to get to know you and you must be prepared to out make that investment in time yourself. Secondly, if you try to rush things you will be taken as just another westerner in a rush who does not understand China. Thirdly, you must be relaxed about revealing those little personal details of family, business and interests which go towards making friends wherever you are. You must also be ready to field very direct personal questions on how much you earn and where you live if you are doing business in the less-developed cities. If you do not feel like answering equally directly then the best way to answer such questions would be to couch your response in terms of what others in Britain would earn and where they too would live. There may well be some sensitivity on the part of your interrogator to provide you with her or his own details due to the different levels of prosperity and living standards in the two countries

Their rules, our rules

Blaise Pascal summed up this quandary very neatly three hundred and fifty years ago when he wrote

Vérité en-deça des Pyrénées, erreur au-delà

Or, what is true on one side of the Pyrenees is a lie on the other. We all act more or less within the same rules as everyone else does within our own society – and so do the Chinese. But, the two sets of rules are very different.

Case Study – Relationship Management and Commitment

Gareth is actively involved in setting up niche training in Shanghai as a natural extension of his highly successful south coast training business. Having formed an alliance with two of his former MBA students, one, Puxi a Shanghai-anese lady with significant work experience in Germany and UK, and Roddie, a fellow Brit who had worked around Greater China for much of his adult life and who had become fascinated by the cross-cultural business. The fourth member was Florian, Puxi's old friend and mentor from the German conglomerate.

Part self-funded and part supported by Gareth, Roddie had carried out detailed market research in Beijing and Shanghai to prove or disprove their business idea; this he did in association with Puxi. The results were similar to what they had hoped for with the exception that the target audience was the young local professional seeking advancement through strategic cross-cultural coaching rather than senior expatriates wanting equally rigorous but less strategic input.

On that basis, the four decided to proceed to the next stage with Gareth and Roddie visiting Shanghai to introduce the former to China and with Puxi's help to prepare and run the first seminar. Key to this was establishing contact with as many influential local business and education personalities.

Disaster struck when Puxi fell victim to a particularly virulent 'flu-like fever just when Roddie was about to set off on his trip and had only partly recovered when Puxi later joined them. Roddie was very frustrated to have wasted 4 days of his 7 day visit without having had the opportunity to sit down with Puxi and work on the programme. Puxi was happy to attend a clinic for four hours each afternoon to get better and the only way they could communicate was by e-mail and mobile 'phone in the evening. He was surprised on the night before I arrived, as the senior partner, to speak to Puxi on her mobile at a social gathering of some kind. 'Oh well' he thought, 'her recovery has been rapid, but that's Chinese medicine for you'.

In view of the value to the enterprise of a well-connected and well-educated Shanghai lady being part of the team, Roddie took a long view.

E-mails regarding Gareth's arrival went unanswered, but Roddie held steady because all 3 were due to meet in his hotel some two hours after Gareth touched down.

Ninety minutes after touchdown, Gareth and Puxi had not appeared for the all-important Welcome to China Meeting. Roddie phoned Puxi, who expressed surprise that his hotel telephone had been engaged and where was he? Did he not know that the venue had been changed to the Imperial Mansion

Hotel, only some two miles across town? Not a problem, said Roddie, grabbing his laptop and jacket, I'll be with you directly.

Matters had moved on by the time that Roddie caught up with them in the opulent lobby of the hotel. Reserved welcomes and bienvenues were exchanged and talks continued. A programme for the week, after he would have to return to UK had been mapped out. None of this was contrary to any of the previous planning discussions, but its encapsulation for Gareth's week was to say the least, skewed.

Over a delicious Thai dinner, Gareth took Roddie to one side and quietly expressed his unease as to the absence of business appointments for the week and concern at Roddie's unspoken discomfort – the pair knew each other well. A useful couple of hours' discussion followed in the lobby of Gareth's apartment block next morning. It appeared that Puxi's father had suffered serious head injuries in a car smash and her daughter's 10th Birthday Party (highly significant locally) had coincided with the visit. Left to their own devices for the rest of the day the pair explored Shanghai's Uighur Quarter and then the illuminated and bustling Bund in the evening as they drew up their plans.

Office politics

Allegiances are formed, split and then reformed in offices in China as anywhere else, but, due to the Confucian influence on society, a schism at the head of division level will carry right down through subordinate staff. Therefore it pays to watch very carefully how the office politics are operating amongst your Chinese partners as you try to move your own strategies forward.

Rivalry

We have already looked at the three concentric rings governing Chinese relationships and it thus follows with such strong bonds that rivalries will be just as strong. These rivalries do not just exist between factions in the office but should your business extend over several cities then do not plan on a great real deal of cooperation between them or not until some considerable time or success has come about.

Checks

Due diligence is not regarded in the same way in China as it is in the West. Because of the deft and, to us, convoluted way in which the Chinese network, they will already know a great deal about the type of people with whom they might be about to do business with and that highly relational assessment is what matters to them rather than stylish company reports. Remember that they have been brought up in a culture of behemoth state-owned enterprises which unsurprisingly reported precisely what the Party and personal ambitions demanded. We must then ask ourselves, post-Enron and post-Shell, which is a more valid approach to checking up on prospective partners?

Chinese communications style and behaviours

If you think communicating with the Chinese is just a languages issue, which can be easily solved with the aid of an interpreter/translator, then you couldn't be more wrong. It can be a slow, laborious activity and fraught with constant dangers in terms of misunderstanding and mistranslation of words, body language and across the cultural subtexts.

In China, when you met a new person, you may often feel you were 'interrogated' with questions which might include:

- your work/job/organization name
- your job title
- how many people work in your company/department/section
- your work at present and in the near future
- your home town and place of work
- your age and experience
- how you dress
- your office
- your car
- your status
- how you are treated by other people
- even, how well you are connected at work and socially.

It is a quicker way for them to find out who you are and if you are worth their while to invest their time and efforts to be one of their guanxi.

Effective communication style

1. Greetings, a few well-chosen Chinese phrases can be most effective.
2. Formality, always use titles until asked not to, especially for the first three times.
3. Communicating effectively with Chinese, speak clearly, slowly and avoid slang.

Recognise that conversation in English with native English speakers can be a strange experience (imagine what it would be like for you speaking in Mandarin to a Chinese person).

Body language

Chinese prefer not to hold eye contact and would rather glance over your eyes, then keep their eyes lowered, usually at the second button of your shirt to show their modesty, especially so if they are ladies.

In China the handshake movement is gentler than in the West.

The importance of silence in conversation cannot be overstated as it is part of the locals' language, to observe and think. What is unsaid, but understood carries more weight than a verbal or written contract.

Placing your right hand over your left fist and raising both hands to your heart is a greeting of respect for the elderly. This is very traditional and will do much to advance relations.

Very much less tactile than ourselves, the Chinese regard touch as quite shocking until friendships have been cemented.

Tips:
- Never use your feet to move an object
- Do not wink or point with your index finger as both are rude gestures
- It is considered improper to put your hand in your mouth.

Establishing rapport

Rapport can be established in just the same way as you would in any new location. You pay attention to what is going on around you and what seems important to your hosts and press ahead. The difference in China is that our two cultures are very different but if you address the strangeness of what surrounds you in terms of the ABC formula then armed with that approach you will quickly learn what is important to those you are dealing with. Whether or not they are fresh-faced young MBAs, tougher businessmen brought up the hard way or party officials, you will know that you need to respect their business cards. Do not be surprised at their combination of group-oriented and individualistic behaviour and their formal way of communicating. Begin by echoing all of this and then you can act as you normally would. Be your normal polite and positive self.

Sharing benefits of training

As a result of the Confucian view that education is all when it comes to personal advancement, then you should not be too surprised when you encounter a strong resistance to the sharing of the information and new skills acquired during training. New initiatives will be proudly rolled out to impress the influential but do not expect tea breaks and meal times to be regaled with the detail of what was learnt. Therefore as a manager you need to decide on how you approach expenditure against company training budgets. What is unkindly known as 'sheep-dip training' whereby you put all your sales team for example through a whole day session, be they 9 or 90 strong, does have one major advantage in China in that all will have been given the same exposure to training and you can be sure that little will be concealed. Individual training will certainly benefit the individual to a far higher degree than in the west and if that is the corporate intention, then that will work.

Case Study A Virtuous Chinese Company

Amongst the rough and tumble along the road to a politically correct form of capitalism, the Weizhi ("Great Aspiration") Group of companies based in the famous city of Xi'an has distinguished itself not only by its profitability but also by its distinct and very traditional corporate culture. A clothing giant with a reputation its products and for treating its customers with respect and fairness, it won the prestigious "1997 Customers' Most Admired Company" from the Quality Association in China. Its operations stretch from its native Shaanxi Province in central China to Inner Mongolia in the north and Guangdong Province in the south with sales of RMB 2 billion. Formed in 1987 by Mr Xiang Bingwei with a small loan, the title of the founder's autobiography gives a clue to his ethos – "My Wealth: Kindness, Sincerity, Wisdom and Diligence". The average education level is post-secondary and average age is 32 with a male/female ratio of 37:29. Not only did Weizhi win the confidence and trust of consumers but it set out to care for its own people through four core beliefs and values: kindness, sincerity, wisdom and diligence – exactly those espoused by Xiang Bingwei. The values which the Group endorses are described as:

- *Love lives – Cherish both time and health*

- *Love oneself – Respect physical and spiritual need, adapt to the society and keep one's individual character simultaneously*

- *Love life – Vigorously create life, realise life and enjoy life in any case*

- *Love career – Love the position, learn, practice, improve and feel happiness when working*

- *Love family members – Respect the old and love the young*

- *Love others – Treat colleagues, friends, customers and the public with fraternity*

- *Love our country – Melt ourselves with the rise and fall of the motherland.*

- *Love the nature – Protect the nature, realize the nature and enjoy the nature – Love the company – Devote yourself to the development of our company, integrate personal improvement and company's development.*

Overlaid on these core beliefs and values are moral maxims such as:

- *Company representatives are exhorted to serve others before themselves and to live the code that those who make others happy are the happiest of all.*

- *Customers are to be served with sincerity*

- *Customers are to be made satisfied*

- *Engage enthusiastically in competition in the marketplace*

- *Provide creative and satisfying products and services to society*

- *To survive and thrive with a sincere heart and diligent hands*

- *To contribute to society with wisdom, knowledge and labour*

- *To accept society's due compensation in the form of fame and profit*

With such formal guidelines and emphasis on social order, the influence of Confucian philosophy on Mr Xiang are clear, as are the rules and regulations of the Legalist school. But the corporate code does not stop there with this combination of the two traditions. Senior managers find that additional codes of conduct are set down for them. The most important of these is "The Three Slaps on the Face". If the senior manager finds that he or she has contravened any of the above four Core Beliefs, if one has not the trust of Weizhi employees or if one is partisan and self-centred. And there is more.

Mr Xiang lives his principles, his people are happy and prosper, and in turn his corporation continues to thrive through demanding adherence to lofty ideals from all. The Weizhi Group is one of China's greatest success stories. Insert whose current sales income is RMB 300 million and tax on sales RMB 30 million winning it the accolade of being one of the "Hundred Strong Company of Selling and Taxing" by the China Costume Association. Their aim is to exceed sales of RMB 500 million by 2015.

10

LEADING MULTICULTURAL TEAMS

The underlying influences of culture, history, geography, ideology, and politics on how the Chinese regard artefacts, behave towards one another and communicate should now be much clearer. You do not need to behave like a local, but with a good grounding in their psyche you can achieve a great deal. The reason that you are in China is for your very foreignness and for what you can bring to the nation with your particular expertise – be it stunning style in the world of fashion, deep IT systems knowledge, the ability to run a manufacturing plant, its complex processes and its people or whatever.

To be really successful in China, as in any foreign environment, you need to be aware not only of the local culture and how that affects people but also of how to operate within that culture. Speaking the local language does help but this cannot always be guaranteed to work, for a few well-chosen phrases is more than enough to get started. Importantly, you need to adapt to cultural differences, find the most effective way to communicate with the local people, be very clear in your own mind about your own ethical values before they are challenged in your new location and above all be open to all that is happening around you so that you can 'read' the business environment accurately using the business acumen with which you arrived.

Adapting to cultural differences

When you arrive in a new country, your senses are immediately bombarded by all that is strange and new, be they different sights such as camels on the Great Wall of China, the sounds of street markets, the smells of new flowers, people who look very different to you, better or worse weather than you are used to and the size difference between British streets and those in the centre of where you find yourself, be it Beijing, Dongguan or Tianjin. All this is very exciting but at the same time a little unsettling. So, your first priority is to get yourself settled into the new environment be it only by snatching a quick moment of peace over a cup of coffee at the airport or resting for your first day in China or indeed going straight out into this fresh melee as soon as you arrive – whichever feels best for you. Whatever you choose does not really matter too much as what you are doing is giving yourself the opportunity to relax into the new setting before having to make difficult or possibly irreversible decisions.

It is quite normal to feel elated and invigorated by your new surroundings for your first few weeks in your new location. Everything seems so different, so exciting, so full of potential and your new team so helpful and focused. As surely as this happens, the opposite then is very likely to happen when you miss all the familiar things at home, what at first sight seemed so different now actually irritates you a little and what you wanted to achieve immediately seems to be dragging on *painfully*. As for your team, the initial positive reception seems to have given way to a sea of troubles and misunderstandings. You should not worry too much about this cultural shock as reason will triumph over emotion and you will settle into a new working routine that will still be very much your own but adapted to the local circumstances. You do not need to ignore all the other expatriates nearby and would be ill advised to do this but you do need to begin to develop acquaintances with the locals as well as with other foreign nationals. By doing this you will not only gain an enormous amount of extra enjoyment from your new location but also show to your team that you have a commitment to them and which they must return in kind. So balance the two, being foreign and accepting the locals as the hosts.

Communicating across cultures

Communicating clearly across different cultures is a critical skill in international business. It involves you putting yourself in the place of the local person with whom you are dealing and working out, all the time, how best to put your message across. In an environment like China, the local staff are unlikely to ask you to repeat things or structure what you say or write more clearly as they will wish to avoid causing you embarrassment at being made to seem a poor communicator and avoid making themselves appear slow in understanding what is required. What will happen is that they will work out for themselves what they think you want and need to have done and do it without any further reference? The answers are to find out to whom you should be speaking in the first place and there your secretary will be of immense help and then secondly find out whether it will be best to make contact face to face, by telephone, by fax, by e-mail or by video conference. All methods have their advantages and disadvantages. Until you get to know your local contacts and they get to know you, face to face meetings are best as they build mutual confidence fastest and allow misunderstandings to be addressed on the spot. Letters and emails are the next favourite since they can be read at leisure and the real meanings made clear. But you need to be especially aware that whilst emails have the great advantage of speed they suffer from a dangerous informality which can cloud intended meanings from non-native English speakers. Telephone calls come in last because they rely solely on the spoken word which may be heavily accented. Telephone calls in a foreign language are very difficult, but if followed with a confirmatory email the aim should be achieved.

In essence, in all cross-cultural communications, be clear in your own mind what it is that you want to put across and then use the clearest and least ambiguous phraseology to do this.

Case study – What should he do?!

John is a very talented middle manager in a large multinational financial services corporation. He joined the Guangzhou office four weeks ago. The new job was very similar to his previous roles. He noticed many of his staff stay in the office very late, often till nearly 10 pm.

He thinks the staff here are over-worked and started staying late himself, lobbying senior management for more staff.

He was wearing himself out with these long working hours and the constant stress of trying to catch up with a seemingly impossible workload.

In modern China, white-collar professionals in big cities often work very late, not always because they have to, it is more so because they want to. For many office workers, home is often a cramped room or rooms where the environment is less comfortable than the office and sometime has no air conditioning.

John should firstly learn more about Chinese cultural and local people live.

Surviving the ethical minefield

It goes without saying that China is not UK nor is UK, China. There are very many different influences at work in both places and it is easy to get confused by 'the way things are done around here'. Your very first step is to rationalize in your own mind why you act ethically in certain ways in the West because before long assaults are likely to be made on your own preconceptions. Your company policy needs to be crystal-clear on this issue as you may need that extra support at some stage. The temptations may come in the form of assurances that business in China only happens via 'brown envelopes', or suggestions that the son of your Deputy General Manager needs your help in some unspecified way to get to a decent university in UK or that it would be a good idea to reward certain members of staff or politicians for services rendered by all-expenses paid trips to Hong Kong or Bangkok. The choice must be yours and so you must have thought this issue through at an early stage so that you remain in control; this is all the more important with the advent of the UK *Bribery Act*.

Good law or bad law it matters nought, the *Bribery Act 2010* is now in force and it impacts immediately on the traditionally effective ways of moving business forward in China. This tome does not set itself up to offer detailed legal advice but rather to provide helpful guidance to those in business with China.

The Act introduced the offence of corporate failure to prevent bribery and extended its reach globally.

The penalties for committing a crime under the Act are severe and its reach global. There is a maximum of 10 years' imprisonment plus an unlimited fine and the potential for the confiscation of property as well as the disqualification of directors. It provides for the prosecution of an individual or company with links to the United Kingdom, regardless of where the crime occurred. It has been described as the toughest anti-corruption legislation in the world with even greater powers than the United States Federal Acquisition Regulations (the FAR) on which it is based. Many are deeply concerned that it criminalises behaviour that is acceptable in the global market and that it will put British business at a competitive disadvantage. Either way it here to stay for the foreseeable future.

So, in this new environment, if you are British and or work for a company with links to the UK then it is critical that not only do you make sure that internal corporate guidance is available to you and your people but because the Act places enormous liability on individuals for compliance, you need a clear grasp on the following key issues regardless of whether your organization operates under English or Scots Law.

To look at this very British Act within the Chinese context the key facets are:

1. The bribery offences. The *Bribery Act* is concerned with 'bribery' and sets this offence apart from other unethical crimes such as fraud, theft, books and records offences. The offence is described as:

   'giving someone a financial or other advantage to encourage that person to perform their functions or activities improperly or to reward that person for having already done so, So this could cover seeking to influence a decision maker by giving some kind of extra benefit to that person.'

   Facilitation payments of any kind are regarded as bribes under the Act.

2. Active and Passive bribery. Active bribery is promising or giving a financial or other advantage. Passive bribery, a newly introduced crime, is agreeing to receive or accepting a financial or other advantage.

3. Bribery of foreign public officials. China has targeted numerous public officials for growing over-rich through office and this has rocked recently the very highest levels of the Chinese Communist Party, so clearly these are sufficiently treacherous waters best avoided at all costs.

4. The failure of commercial organisations to prevent bribery by an associated person acting on your behalf but only if that person performs services for you. However this corporate offence is unlikely to place liability on you if that person is simply a supplier. If however you are setting up a network or new business it pays to pay extremely close attention to what associates may be doing in your names. Be very concerned if such people are paying an unapproved 'fee' or facilitation payment to progress your business – you might well find a copy-cat firm operating under your own name as did Apple in a very sophisticated branding scam.

This is all pretty dry stuff but by this stage you should have formed a pretty good opinion of what this new law is all about.

There is however some glimmer of light for the business person in China in that the Act clearly states that hospitality is not prohibited and that:

'any hospitality should reflect a desire to cement good relations and show appreciation, and that promotional expenditure should seek to improve the image of [a company] as a commercial organisation, to better present its products or services, or establish cordial relations.'

There is however a caveat as one would expect:

'the recipient should not be given the impression that they are under an obligation to confer any business advantage or that the recipient's independence will be affected.'

So long as the level of entertainment is considered "appropriate, reasonable and proportionate" and is monitored, the terms of the Act should be satisfied. Do however be very careful should a supplier relationship exist.

As with all UK businesses operating overseas you and your organization need to make sure that:

- clear company policy on Bribery is in place which contains guidance on levels of appropriate expenditure on gifts and entertainment.
- A senior executive is given responsibility for this matter.
- Records are kept of associated expenditure.
- Staff are trained in best practice.
- A risk assessment has been made for your operations.

The Act will doubtless place UK businesses at an initial disadvantages across China until it is realized and accepted that these changes in behaviour are a consequence of government and not company policy. You can pre-empt much of this damage yourself in discussions with your Chinese counterparts making it quite clear that bound though you are by the UK *Bribery Act* you want to do good business within its strictures – the Chinese know all about regulations and how to work with them.

Case study – do not get involved in corruption and illegal activities

An investment deal of $19.5 billion between two Chinese state-owned aluminium firms, one the second largest mining company in the world, collapsed. One employee was later sentenced in prison for 10 years for accepting bribes.

Most foreigners are led to believe that this is typical 杀鸡吓猴 (shājī xiàhóu) – warning the many by punishing a few well known wrong-doers and that was why they were made an example of.

People think corruption is common in China, but corruption is illegal as anywhere else. If foreign companies get caught, the reality can be harsh.

Moving on/recovering from serious gaffes

To return to matters more cross-cultural, if you do become aware that you have caused some offence, a swift apology and return to business matters will normally suffice. If however a loss of Face has been caused it is vital that you find a go-between, fast, to rebuild the relationship otherwise your whole team will be destabilised by, what to a Westerner, was a trivial incident. In so doing you are not in the least taking away from your own managerial authority, rather paying swift and sensitive attention to a local cultural issue of great importance.

Individual priorities

As in any office there will be individual priorities but as elsewhere local culture does not dictate that these take precedence over corporate needs. By getting to know your managers and staff, they too will come to know and respect you. The simple expedient of getting out of your own office to chat to your people at their own workplaces works as well in China as it does anywhere else in breaking down barriers and building a fully-functioning team. A great many misunderstandings can be forestalled in general conversation before they grow out of proportion. If you are approached to assist in personal matters then it is best to suggest that the supplicant applies in the normal way otherwise you will have a stream of such requests coming your way, line managers will lose Face and an unhappy office will result.

Time

There are very different Asian and European views of time but the Chinese have a highly developed sense of punctuality and that is one less thing to worry about in China. If anything, you will need to pay rather more attention to getting to meetings on time in China than in UK where often late trains and busy motorways are acceptable excuses for running behind schedule. In a country which has had appalling roads and transport for generations, the Chinese allow plenty of time for delays and demand that punctuality of business associates. They will happily wait in a car until the due time to alight and so arrive on time and see no reason why others should not do exactly the same.

Rudeness

As in any multinational or multinational situation, the potential always exists for misunderstanding to arise and more often than not unintentional rudeness. You should not be too sensitive when you are bombarded with very direct personal questions as rudeness is not intended merely information gathering as the Chinese begin to get to know you. If there are some things which you really view as far too personal to discuss early on in relationships, then it pays to have a ready stock of politely deflecting comments to the effect that what you earn is much the same as other international business people and that the villa or hotel that you are staying in is covered by your company and not really symbolic of any personal wealth and so on. If however it is you who has been really rude in error, an immediate apology will restore harmony to the meeting. There is a positive here and that is that as the Chinese come to regard you as a friend they become more and more direct and in casting off their highly structure politeness they are in fact paying you a great compliment.

Case study – Say please and thank you?!

Zhang has been friends with Ron for nearly three months, they started really well, but were getting quite frustrated with their friendship.

Zhang stopped saying please and thank you to Ron, when he helped her out. He feels Zhang is taking him for granted and being rather rude.

While Zhang thinks Ron is being rather distant to her, he says please and thank you all the time, even for a cup of tea.

Among friends and family, the Chinese way of being polite to each other with words is to shorten the social distance between you. Saying please and thanks all the time serves to insert a kind of buffer or space. It has the effect of placing formality between friends.

Making culture work for business success

Foreign visitors can be surprised to discover the extent to which their Chinese business contact will make an effort to keep them entertained at all times. In China a host's responsibility includes fulfilling all needs and ensuring that the comfort, care and protection of their guests is attended to. If you wish to spend some time alone, indicate so very politely, or make a plan before arrive in China, so your host knows you are not under their 'care' at your planed time.

Reading the local business environment

By following the above guidelines and using what you have learnt about the drivers of Chinese business culture you are well on the way to getting to grips with what is happening in your new environment and of course you should not aim at being totally self-reliant in this respect. Your own network will give you as much information as you yourself put in. In the tough business world of China everyone else is working hard to find out what is really happening and mingling with local expatriates will provide a lot of useful information.

Cultural Banana Skins

There are a few areas to avoid if you want to keep relationships harmonious with the Chinese. Firstly, do not draw them out on politics, religion or the Chinese Communist Party because that could well lead to unwelcome awkwardness.

Secondly, be mindful of Face and causing loss of Face. Just be rather more considerate than you need to be in the west.

If you promote a dynamic, well (Western) educated young person to a very senior position too quickly, it may not always work out well. Respecting the hierarchy of Chinese society / company is important. You may need to take your time in promoting him / her to that stage where others show this person respect in light of his/her ability for do the job as well as keeping the atmosphere harmonious in the company.

Apart from that there is no real mystery. If you just be your normal polite western self, then the Chinese will respect that for itself.

The eight key ways in which to manage in China

1. Embrace local culture
2. Build relationships
3. Seek local assistance to gain cultural knowledge
4. Help Chinese employees understand you
5. Adapt products and practices to local markets
6. Coordinate by region in China
7. Remember the pace of development in China is relentless – there is greater understanding and appreciation of the Western way of doing business
8. The Gap is however still WIDE.

11

CHINESE LANGUAGE

The Chinese language includes Mandarin 普通话 (pǔtōnghuà), the common Speech, 汉语 (Hànyǔ), and Han Chinese language known as either 华语 (Huáyǔ) or 中文 (Zhōngwén). Chinese is a language family of seven main mutually unintelligible dialects from different parts of the country. For example, Cantonese and Taishanese are mainly spoken in Guangdong and by most overseas Chinese and Wu is spoken by Shanghainese and Han Yu is the preeminent form at this moment. Chinese is spoken natively in China, Taiwan, Singapore, and other places with Chinese communities such as Malaysia, the United States, Canada, Philippines, Australia, Thailand, Vietnam, Indonesia, Mauritius and Peru, by about 1.5 billion people on the planet. It is also an official language in United Nations.

The written language was a great unifying element for all Chinese when there was no common language and the Chinese feel a great affection for these very old written friends. There are well over 20,000 characters, of which roughly 8,000 would be used by a well-educated Chinese person today. To read a Chinese newspaper you need to know about 3,000, and 1,200 would be enough to get the gist. However Chinese characters should not be confused with Chinese words as most Chinese vocabularies are made up of two different characters. Chinese characters evolved over time from earlier forms of hieroglyphs. The idea that all Chinese characters are either pictographs or ideographs is an erroneous one: most characters are composites of phonetic and semantic radicals.

The Korean, Japanese, and Vietnamese languages have been greatly influenced by Chinese culture throughout the history. Korean and Japanese both have writing systems employing Chinese characters, called Hanja and Kanji, respectively. The Vietnamese term for Chinese writing is known as Han too.

The modern Romanisation that has been used in this book is known as Pinyin. It was first adopted in the 1958s by the Chinese government and it became official in 1979.

Pinyin

In Mandarin, pinyin literally means 'spell of sound', it is a system using Romanised Alphabet (25 letters out of 26 are used, except letter 'v') and four accents over the letters indicate which of the 4 tones should be used. There are 6 basic vowels and 21 consonants in Chinese Pinyin. A syllable always consists of a vowel or a consonant with a vowel. Vowels can stand by themselves when no initial consonant is present.

Tones

Mandarin is a tonal language. The tones are represented as follows:

First tone: —
Second tone: /
Third tone: v
Fourth tone: \
Neutral tone: o

Pinyin syllables are made up of initials (vowels) and finals (consonants). But what do these tones sound like? English uses tones too, so they should not be too hard to master. Here is a graphic representation of the sound of each tone:

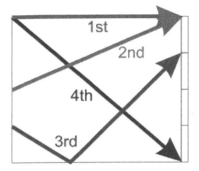

Tone	Mark	Description
1st	mā	High and level.
2nd	má	Starts medium in tone, then rises to the top.
3rd	mǎ	Starts low, dips to the bottom, then rises toward the top.
4th	mà	Starts at the top, then falls sharp and strong to the bottom.
Neutral	ma	Flat, pronounced very weakly.

Initials (vowels)

The following vowels will be read in the first tone. The first tone is like singing a sustained note. If you read them in the following order, you will notice that the gap between your lips will gradually get narrower.

The six vowels in Pinyin ā, ō, ē, ī, ū and ǖ in the first tone:

ā – Open your mouth wide and say: "aah".

ō – Push your lips forward into a small circle, with your tongue at the bottom of your mouth, leaving a hollow space above it. Say: "o". Your lips should make the shape they take when you say the English word "law".

ē – Make a sound as if you have seen something really disgusting: "ergh". When e is used with other vowels it can also be pronounced "ê" which is similar to "e" in the English word "bed".

ī —   Pull your lips slightly back and push your tongue up towards the hard palate without touching it. It is similar to the "ea" sound in the English word "eat".

ū —   Push your lips forward and make a narrow gap through which your breath can vibrate. Your lips should take the shape they make when you say the word "fool".

ǖ —   It is similar to the umlaut "ü" in German or the French "u". Say "ee" through tightly pursed lips (form the shape they make when you say the "sh" of the English word fish).

Finals (consonants)

There are 21 initials in Chinese. Most words in Pinyin are pronounced as they would be in English pronunciations. However there are some which are not, and in a few cases, the sounds used in English do not occur in Chinese, so their representative letters have been adopted for other sounds.

The following consonants are similar to their English equivalents:

f, k, l, m, n, p, s, t, w, y

The following consonants are not unfamiliar sounds to speakers of English:

b —   like p in spare
d —   like t in stand
g —   like g in girl

These consonant sounds are more difficult:

c —   like ts in cats
ch —   like ch in chair, but with the mouth in a round shape and the tongue further back
h —   like h in him but with a bit more fiction in the throat (not as much as in Scottish loch)
j —   like j in joke but with the tongue nearer the teeth
q —   like ch in chair, but with the tongue further forward

r –   like r in rough, but with the tongue curled upwards
sh –   like sh in ship
x –   between s and sh, though there is no sound in English which
       is the same as the sound x in Chinese. Place the front of
       your tongue behind the lower front teeth, then let the air
       pass through.
z –   like ds in lads
zh –   like j in jump, but with the tongue further back

Vowels and vowel combinations

a –   like a in bath
ai –   like ie in pie, or eye
ao –   like ow in cow
e –   like ur in fur (without rolling the r)
ei –   like ay in May
er –   similar to 'are' when said in an Irish accent
i –   like ee in bee after most letters, BUT
i –   after s, z, r, c, sh, ch, zh, it sounds more like
               'uh', and serves to lengthen the sound of those
               consonant preceding it.
ia / ya –   combine i and a, like ya in Yahoo
iao / yao –   combine i and ao, like yow in yowl
ie / ye –   like ye in yellow
iu / yu –   like yo in yo-yo
ian / yan –   like yen, the Japanese currency
iang / yang – combine i and ang, like yan in yank
iong / yong – combine i and ong
o –   like o in more
ou –   like oa in boat
ong –   like ong in song
u –   like u in flute, BUT when after j, q, x or y it sounds
               like the u sound in French tu
ü –   like the u sound in French tu
ua / wa –   combine u and a
uo / wo –   combine u and o
uai / wai –   combine u and ai

uan /wan –   combine u and an
un –   like oon in spoon, but said faster
uang / wang –   combine u and ang, like wang in wangle

Basic Grammar

Mandarin grammar is relatively straightforward.

1. There are no verb conjugations for different tenses, singular or plural, or gender.

2. There are no articles (a/an/the).

3. At a basic level, sentence order is similar to that of English:

subject-verb-object

For example,

I study Chinese.
(literally: I – study – Chinese)
Wǒ xué Hànyǔ.
我 学 汉语。

I studied Chinese.
('le' is the past particle indicating an action happened in the past or completed)
Wǒ xué le Hànyǔ.
我 学 了 汉语。

I'm learning Chinese.
(zài indicates an action is ongoing)
Wǒ zài xué Hànyǔ.
我 在 学 汉语。

4. How to form a simple 'yes/no' question?

a) A very simple way to form a question in Chinese is by putting a question particle "ma" at the end of a sentence that would otherwise be a plain statement. For example,

Do you learn Chinese?
Nǐ xué Hànyǔ ma?
你 学 汉语 吗？

b) An affirmative-negative question is another way of asking question. The word "bù" means not, it is a negative word.

Do you, don't you learn Chinese?
Nǐ xué bù xué Hànyǔ?
你 学 不 学 汉语？

5. So how do you ask 'what'?

什么 (Shénme) is the interrogative word "what" The most important feature about Chinese interrogative pronouns is that, unlike English practice, which shifts all interrogative pronouns to the beginning of the question, Chinese keeps them in the position in the sentence where the answers would be expected. For example,

What do you study?
(literally: you – study – what?)
Nǐ xué shénme?
你 学 什么？

6. So how do you ask 'where'?

哪里 (Nǎlǐ) is the interrogative word "where". For example,

Where do you live? (literally: you – live – at – where?)
Nǐ zhù zài nǎlǐ?
你 住 在 哪里？

7. So how do you ask 'which'?

哪 (Nǎ) is the interrogative word "which". For example,

What nationality are you?
(literally: you – are – which – country – person?)
Nǐ shì nǎ guó rén?
你 是 哪 国 人？

TOPIC 1
GREETINGS

English	Chinese Characters	Pinyin*	Notes
Hello/Hi	你好	nǐ hǎo	
Good morning	早上好	zǎo shàng hǎo	
Good afternoon	下午好	xià wǔ hǎo	
Good evening	晚上好	wǎn shàng hǎo	
Welcome!	欢迎光临!	huān yíng guāng lín!	Formal
How are you?	你好吗?	nǐ hǎo ma	
I am fine	我很好	wǒ hěn hǎo	
Thank you	谢谢	xiè xie	
You're welcome!	不客气	bú kè qì	Standard reply for thank you
Sorry/excuse me	对不起	duì bù qǐ	
Never mind	没关系	méi guān xì	Standard reply for sorry
Good night	晚安	wǎn ān	
Good bye	再见	zài jiàn	

Pinyin words in these tables are broken down into separate units to correspond to each individual Chinese character for readability for total beginners.

Vocabulary

English	Chinese Characters	Pinyin	Notes
Good	好	hǎo	
Not	不	bù / bú	Not good: 不好
To be (am / are / is / was / were …)	是	shì	
Is not	不是	bú shì	
Morning	早上	zǎo shàng	
Afternoon	下午	xià wǔ	
Evening	晚上	wǎn shàng	
You	你	nǐ	
You	您	nín	More polite and formal
Question particle words	吗	ma	
Very	很	hěn	
Thank	谢谢	xiè xie	
Polite / courteous / formal	客气	kè qì	
Content / calm / quiet / to find a place for / peace	安	ān	
To see / to meet	见	jiàn	
Again / once more	再	xài	

- "Nǐ hǎo". This is a common, slightly formal, greeting. The response is usually simply "nǐ hǎo" again.

- "Nǐ hǎo ma?" Literally it would translate as "How are you?", however, it is not really a question. The response is usually "wǒ hěn hǎo, xiè xie." *I'm very well, thanks.*

- Personal pronouns:
  There is no distinction for case. wǒ is wǒ regardless of whether it is the subject of the sentence or the object of the verb, and the same is true for the second and third person pronouns. Nor is there a distinction for gender except in the written form as shown below. tā is tā, whether it refers to a woman or a man.

Singular
Personal pronouns use the same form regardless of being subject or object, for example I or me for 我 (wǒ).

First person singular: 我 (wǒ) – I, me
Second person singular: 你 (nǐ) – you
Third person singular, masculine: 他 (tā) – he, him
Third person singular, feminine: 她 (tā) – she, her

Plural
For plural forms by adding the plural marker 们 (men)

First person plural: 我们 (wǒmen) – we, us
Second person plural: 你们 (nǐmen) – you (all)
Third person plural, masculine or mixed: 他们 (tāmen) – they, them
Third person plural, feminine: 她们 (tāmen) – they, them
Teacher 老师 (lǎo shī)
Teachers 老师们 (lǎo shī men)

TOPIC 2
INTRODUCTION

English	Chinese Characters	Pinyin	Notes
May I (Let's me) introduce myself?	让我自我介绍一下？	ràng wǒ zì wǒ jiè shào yí xià?	一下 shows that an action lasts for a very short time.
I am /called Ming Wang.	我是/叫王明。	wǒ shì / jiào Wáng Míng.	Wang is the family name, Ming is the first name.
I work for Apple, I'm marketing manager. How about you?	我为苹果工作，我是市场部经理。您呢？	wǒ wèi Píng guǒ gōng zuò, wǒ shì shì chǎng bù jīng lǐ. nín ne?	
Hello, Mr Wang.	你好，王先生。	nǐ hǎo, Wáng xiān shēng.	
My surname is Li, I'm called Ming Li.	我姓李，我叫李明。	wǒ xìng Li, wǒ jiào Lǐmíng.	
I work for Microsoft, I'm a software engineer.	我为微软工作，我是一个软件工程师。	wǒ wèi Wēi ruǎn gōng zuò, wǒ shì yī gè ruǎn jiàn gōng chéng shī.	
This is my business card.	这是我的名片。	zhè shì wǒ de míng piàn.	
I'm British.	我是英国人。	wǒ shì Yīng guó rén.	
Nice to meet you.	很高兴认识你。	hěn gāo xìng rèn shi nǐ.	
Nice to meet you too.	我也很高兴认识你。	wǒ yě hěn gāo xìng rèn shi nǐ.	

Who is that?	那是谁?	nà shì shuí?	
This is my managing director.	这是我的董事长。	zhè shì wǒ de dǒngshì zhǎng.	
Is (or isn't) he an American?	他是不是美国人?	tā shì bù shì Měi guó rén?	
What is your (precious) surname?	您贵姓?	nín guì xìng?	Formal, and more common for first time meetings
What is your name (you called)?	你叫什么?	nǐ jiào shén me?	Casual way of asking name

Vocabulary

English	Chinese Characters	Pinyin	Notes
Introduce	介绍	jiè shào	
Oneself	自己	zì jǐ	
Self-introduction	自我介绍	zì wǒ jiè shào	
For/to/in order to	为	wèi	
Yourself	你自己	nǐ zì jǐ	
Myself	我自己	wǒ zì jǐ	
Happy	高兴	gāo xìng	
To know	认识	rèn shi	
What	什么	shén me	

Names	姓名	xìng míng	
Business card	名片	míng piàn	
Britain	英国	Yīng guó	
China	中国	Zhōng guó	
People	人	rén	
Chinese	中国人	Zhōng guó rén	nationality
Is	是	shì	
Not	不	bù/ bú	
Sir/Mr	先生	xiān shèng	
Madam/Lady/Ms	女士	nǚ shì	
Miss	小姐	xiǎo jiě	
This	这	zhè	
That	那	nà	

- In a Chinese name, the surname or family name always comes first, followed by the given name. Most surnames consist of a single character, though some have two. Given names may be either one or two characters. Depending on social circumstances, individuals identify themselves either

   a) by surname only: Wǒ xìng Zhāng (my surname is Zhang)

   or

   b) by full name: Wǒ jiào Zhāng Wěi, or Wǒ shì Zhāng Wěi. (jiào – called; shì – is)

- Predicative verb or adjective can be used. For example is or isn't 是不是 can be used to make an inquiry:

Are you, are you not English?

你是不是英国人?

Nǐ shìbúshì yīngguó rén?

Exception: good or not good 好不好, and is always placed at the end of the sentence, means "OK?".

- Adding 呢 (ne) marker at end of a statement to make when repeating same question, or a question about a different subject, or used to indicate the continuous characteristic of an action / situation. It can be suggestive or a hint of doubt.

TOPIC 3
NUMBERS

English	Chinese Characters	Pinyin	Notes
Your seat number?	你的座位是几号？	nǐ de zuò wèi shì jǐ hào?	
Number 8.	第八号。	dì bā hào.	
What is the population of China (how many people does China has)?	中国有多少人口？	Zhōng guó yǒu duō shǎo rénkǒu?	
1,339,724,852	十三亿三千九百七十二万四千八百五十二个人	shí sān yì sān qiān jiǔ bǎi qī shí èr wàn sì qiān bā bǎi wǔ shí èr gè rén	
How much is this please?	请问，这个多少钱？	qǐng wèn, zhè ge duō shǎo qián?	
Ten Yuan.	十块／元。	shí kuài / yuán。	Yuan is more formal, Kuai is used in spoken form
I want this one. Thanks.	我要这个。谢谢。	wǒ yào zhè ge. xiè xiè.	
How old are you?	你多大？	nǐ duō dà?	
I'm 18.	我十八岁了。	wǒ shí bā suì le.	
How old are you?	你几岁？	nǐ jǐ suì?	Only used to ask a child
I am six.	六岁。	liù suì.	

Vocabulary

English	Chinese Characters	Pinyin	Notes
Zero	零	líng	
One	一	yī	
Two	二 / 两	èr / liǎng	When counting, two is 二 (èr), when used with measure words, it is 两 (liǎng)
Three	三	sān	
Four	四	sì	
Five	五	wǔ	
Six	六	liù	
Seven	七	qī	
Eight	八	bā	
Nine	九	jiǔ	
Ten	十	shí	
Hundred	百	bǎi	
Thousand	千	qiān	
Ten thousand	万	wàn	10,000
One hundred million	亿	yì	100,000,000

How many/ much?	几	jǐ	Used for small numbers – can be replied with 'a few' in English. Another meaning is 'several'.
How many/ much?	多少	duō shǎo	There is no such distinction between many and much in Chinese.
Ordinal Number	第	dì	The first is 第一 (dì yī) Second 第二 (dì èr)
Measure word	个	gè	
This	这	zhè	
Age	岁	suì	
How old	多大	duō dà	

- The Chinese number system is simple and generally easy to learn. Multiples of 10 are made by stating the multiple and then 10. Thus 20 is literally "two ten." If you learn the numbers from one to 10, you can count to 100 without having to learn any new vocabulary. The Chinese counting system is based on units of 10.

Numbers 11-99:
11 is 10 and 1 – shí yī
22 is 2 X10, and 2 – èr shí èr
90 is 9 X 10 – jiǔ shí
99 is 9 X10, and 9 – jiǔ shí jiǔ

Numbers 101-999
101 – yī bǎi líng yī
111 – yī bǎi yī shí yī
999 – 9X100, 9X10, and 9 – jiǔ bǎi jiǔ shǐ jiǔ

Numbers 1001-9999
1001 – yī qiān líng yī (only need to say one zero)
1010 – yī qiān líng shí
9999 – 9X1000, 9X100, 9X10 and 9 – jiǔ qiān jiǔ bǎi jiǔ shí jiǔ

- Ordinal numbers: add a prefix of 第 (dì) at the front of a number, and it becomes an ordinal. For example:

First – 第一 (dì'yī)
Second – 第二 (dì'èr)
10th – 第十 (dì shí)

- Measure words also known as classifiers or count words and are used along with numerals to define the size and shape of a given object, or with "this"/"that" to identify specific object, it is like the 'cup' in a cup of tea, the 'bottle' in two bottles of beer in English. Most generic measure word is 个 (gè). For example, two people 两个人.

TOPIC 4
ASKING THE DATE, YEAR, MONTH, DATE OR DAY

English	Chinese Characters	Pinyin	Notes
What day is today?	今天(是)几号?	jīn tiān (shì) jǐ hào?	shì is usually omitted.
(It's) Thursday, 3rd May 2013.	(今天是)二零一三年五月三日/号，星期四。	(jīn tiān shì) èr líng yī sān nián wǔ yuè sān rì / hào, xīng qī sì.	In year, month and date sequence, and the year is in single digits when speaking
What day of the week is tomorrow?	明天星期几?	míng tiān xīng qī jǐ?	
(It's) Friday	星期五	xīng qī wǔ.	
When are you going to China?	你什么时候去中国?	nǐ shén me shí hou qù Zhōng guó?	shén me shí hou means when
Next month.	下个月。	xià gè yuè.	
How long for?	去多长时间?	qù duō cháng shí jiān?	
Five days.	五天。	wǔ tiān.	
I am going to work tomorrow.	我明天(要去)上班。	wǒ míng tiān (yào qù) shàng bān.	上班 (shàngbān) means go to work
I go to work today.	我今天(去)上班。	wǒ jīn tiān qù shàng bān.	
I went to work yesterday.	我昨天去上班了。	wǒ zuó tiān qù shàng bān le.	
Tomorrow I go to work.	明天我去上班。	míng tiān wǒ qù shàng bān.	

Vocabulary

English	Chinese Characters	Pinyin	Notes
Week	星期	xīng qī	
Day	天	tiān	
Date	日/号	rì / hào	Number + ri E.g. èr shí liú rì/二十六日/26th
Month	月	yuè	Number + yuè e.g. sān yuè 三月/March
Year	年	nián	
Today	今天	jīn tiān	
Tomorrow	明天	míng tiān	
Yesterday	昨天	zuó tiān	
To go	去	qù	
Last year	去年	qù nián	
This year	今年	jīn nián	
Next year	明年	míng nián	
Every	每	měi	
This month/week	这个月/星期	zhè gè yuè/xīng qī	
Last month/week	上个月/星期	shàng gè yuè/xīng qī	
Next month/week	下个月/星期	xià gè yuè/xīng qī	

Going to / want to	要 + Verb	yào	
Date	号 / 日	hào/ rì	

- In Chinese the date follows a year, month and date sequence.

- The year is in single digit number plus the year when speaking. For example, the year 2013 – 二零一三年 (èr líng yī sān nián).

- For months, they are numbered from 1 to 12 plus the month word for Jan to Dec. For example, May – 五月 (wǔ yuè).

- The date is numbered 1-31 plus the day word, for example, 3ʳᵈ – 三号 (sān hào) or 三日 (sān rì). 三号 (sān hào) is used more often when speaking.

- Days of the week are 'week' plus number 1-6 for Mon to Sat, Monday is literally 'week one', Tuesday is 'week two' and Thursday is 星期四 (xīng qī sì). Sunday is 星期天 (xīng qī tiān) / 日 (rì).

- Verbs have only ONE form regardless of the time of action – past, present or future, for example, yesterday, today or tomorrow. To indicate tense, time referenced words such as "yesterday", "today" and "tomorrow" are added before or after the subject. In addition some modal particles are used such as 要 (yào) or 了 (lè), see below.

- Add 要 (yào) before a verb, means want to or going to do something.

- 了 (lè) is added after a verb such as 了 or at an end of sentences, to indicate that an action is completed, or situation has changed.

- Month and Week are often used with a numeral-measure word 个.

- Time periods: five days 五天 (wǔ tiān), 2 hours 两个小时 (liǎng gè xiǎoshí), three years 三年 (sān nián).

TOPIC 5
TELLING THE TIME

English	Chinese Characters	Pinyin	Notes
What time is it (now)?	现在几点了？	xiàn zài jǐ diǎn le.	
Two o'clock.	两点。	liǎng diǎn.	
It is 2:10.	两点十分。	liǎng diǎn shí fēn.	
It is 2:30.	两点半。	liǎng diǎn bàn.	
When do you finish work?	你几点下班？	nǐ jǐ diǎn xià bān?	
I finish work on 5pm.	我下午5点下班。	wǒ xià wǔ wǔ diǎn xià bān.	

Vocabulary

English	Chinese Characters	Pinyin	Notes
Hour	点	diǎn	
Hour	小时	xiǎo shí	
Minute	分	fēn	
Second	秒	miǎo	

Now	现在	xiàn zài	
Morning	上午	shàng wǔ	
Afternoon	下午	xià wǔ	
Evening	晚上	wǎn shàng	
Half	半	bàn	
Finish work	下班	xià bān	

TOPIC 6
ASKING FOR DIRECTIONS

English	Chinese Characters	Pinyin	Notes
Excuse me, where is the toilet?	对不起，洗手间在哪里？	duì bù qǐ, xǐ shǒu jiān zài nǎ lǐ?	... zài nǎ lǐ?
Over here / there.	在那里/这里。	zài nà lǐ/zhè lǐ.	
How do I get to The Beijing Hotel?	怎么去北京饭店？	zěn me qù Běijīng fàn diàn?	
Turn left at the second road, then go straight on, it's on your right hand side.	第二条路左拐，然后一直向前走，它在你的右边。	dì èr tiáo lù zuǒ guǎi, rán hòu yī zhí xiàng qián zǒu, tā zài nǐ de yòu biān.	
Are there any internet cafes nearby?	附近有网吧吗？	fùjìn yǒu wǎng bā ma?	
I will go by bus / taxi / drive.	我坐车/坐出租/开车去。	wǒ zuò chē / zuò chū zū / kāi chē qù.	

Vocabulary

English	Chinese Characters	Pinyin	Notes
Entrance	入口	rù kǒu	
Exit / export	出口	chū kǒu	
Left	左	zuǒ	

Right	右	yòu	
Turn	转	zhuǎn	
Turn left	左转	zuǒ zhuǎn	
Turn right	右转	yòu zhuǎn	
Front	前	qián	
Back	后	hòu	
East	东（边）	dōng (bian)	
West	西	xī	
North	北	běi	
South	南	nán	
Step	步	bù	
To walk	步行	bù xíng	
By (car)	坐	zuò	
Car，Bus	车	chē	
By bus	坐车	zuò chē	
Stop	站	zhàn	
Metro	地铁	dìtiě	
Straight	直行	zhí xíng	
Traffic light	红绿灯	hóng lǜ dēng	Red-green lights

Entrance	入口	rù kǒu	入 is enter, 口 is mouth
Exit	出口	chū kǒu	
Opposite	对面	duì miàn	
To across	过	guò	
Road	马路	mǎ lù	
Cross the road	过马路	guò mǎ lù	
Distance	距离	jiù lí	
To operate (vehicle)	开	kāi	
By car	开车	kāi chē	
Movie	电影	diàn yǐng	
Cinema	电影院	diàn yǐng yuàn	
(located) at / in / exist/over	在	zài	
Internet cafe	网吧	wǎng bā	
Inside	里	lǐ	

- 在 (zài), one of the meanings is 'at', used to indicate a location. For example, the toilet is here 洗手间在这里 (xǐ shǒu jiān zài zhè lǐ).). It can also be used to form a question by adding the question word 吗 at the end to form a simple Yes/No question. For example, Is there a toilet here? 洗手间在这里吗? (Xǐ shǒu jiān zài zhè lǐ ma?)

  For example, is the toilet here? 洗手间在这里吗? (xǐ shǒu jiān zài zhè lǐ ma?)

TOPIC 7
SHOPPING

English	Chinese Characters	Pinyin	Notes
I'm thinking about buying a pair of new shoes.	我想买一双新鞋。	wǒ xiǎng mǎi yì shuāng xīn xié.	一双 A pair
I want to buy this computer.	我要买这个电脑。	wǒ yào mǎi zhè gè diàn nǎo.	
How much Is it?	多少钱？	duō shǎo qián?	
In total 3256.87 Yuan.	一共三千二百五十六元/块八角/毛七分。	yī gòng sān qiān èr bǎi wǔ shí liù yuán/kuài bā jiǎo/máo qī fēn.	
It is too expensive!	太贵了！	tài guì le!	
May I have discount?	能便宜点么？	néng pián yí diǎn me?	
OK, 3,000 Kuai	好，三千块。	hǎo, sān qiān kuài.	
I don't have that much cash.	我没有那么多的现金。	wǒ méi yǒu nà me duō de xiàn jīn.	
This is my credit card.	这是我的信用卡。	zhè shì wǒ de xìn yòng kǎ.	
Please may I have receipt?	请给我收据好吗？	qǐng gěi wǒ shōu jù hǎo ma?	

Vocabulary

English	Chinese Characters	Pinyin	Notes
To sell/buy	买/卖	mǎi/mài	mǎi mài means business
Expensive/cheap	贵/便宜	guì/pián yí	
Want	要	yào	
Looking for	找	zhǎo	
Have a look	看看	kàn kan	
Try something on	试试	shì shi	
Size	号码	hào mǎ	
Money	钱	qián	
Price	价格	jià gé	
Pay by cash/card	付现金/信用卡	fù xiàn jīn/xìn yòng kǎ	
Receipt	收据	shōu jù	
Password	密码	mì mǎ	
Colour	颜色	yán sè	
Too big/too small	太大 / 太小	tài dà/tài xiǎo	
(the size) is just right	合适	hé shì	
Good quality / bad quality	质量好/质量差	zhì liàng hǎo/zhì liàng chà	

Discount	折扣	zhé kòu	
Return	退货	tuì huò	
Exchange	换	huàn	
Need/or not	需(要)不需要	xū (yào) bù xū yào	
Want/or not want	想(要)不想要	xiǎng (bù) xiǎng yào	
May	可不可以	kě bù kě yǐ	
A cup of tea	一杯茶	yī bēi chá	
One piece of clothing	一件衣服	yī jiàn yī fú	

- The unit of Chinese currency RMB 元/角/分 Yuán/jiǎo/fēn, in spoken form

块 毛 分	kuài máo fēn	
元 / 块	yuán / kuài	(unit of money, yuán)
角 / 毛	jiǎo / máo	(a unit of money, 0.1 yuán)
分	fēn	(a unit of money, 0.1 máo)

  The current exchange rate is about £1.00 = 9 元 (yuán) 8 角 (jiǎo) 7 分 (fēn) (CNY 9.87).

- A noun followed by 的 (de) indicates possession. For example my 我的 (wǒ de); teacher's money 老师的钱 (lǎoshī de qián).

- A verb can be repeated to indicate that the action is of a very short duration, for example

  Have a look – 看看 (kàn kan)

  It also softens the tone or makes it sound relaxed or informal.

- Helping verbs such as can / able to 会 (huì), would like to 想 (xiǎng), want 要 (yào), should 应该 (yīng gāi), and must 必须 (bì xūare) more often than not appear before verbs to express ability, possibility, intention, wishes.

- 多 (duō) as an approximate indicator of number, may be used between a measure word and a noun, or after a measure-noun, to express the remainder of a round figure.

- In Chinese, with a common noun (name of objects) used with a numeral, the numeral has to have a measure word between it and the noun. gè is by far the most common measure word and it can occur with a wide range of nouns. For example,

a cup of tea, 一杯茶 (yì bēi chá)
two bottles of beer, 两瓶啤酒 (liǎng píng píjiǔ)
three (plates of) dishes 三盘菜 (sān pán cài)
ten cities 十个城市 (shí gè chéngshì).

TOPIC 8
EATING OUT IN A RESTAURANT

English	Chinese Characters	Pinyin	Notes
I like Chinese food / Western food.	我喜欢中国菜/西餐。	wǒ xǐ huan Zhōng guó cài / xīcān.	
Please give me a menu.	请给我菜单。	qǐng gěi wǒ cài dān.	
What would you like to eat / drink?	你想吃/喝什么？	nǐ xiǎng chī / hē shén me?	
I would like to have the beef vegetables stir-fry.	我要牛肉炒青菜。	wǒ yào niú ròu chǎo qīng cài.	
Steamed fish please.	要清蒸鱼。	yào qīng zhēng yú.	
I am a vegetarian.	我吃素。	wǒ chī sù.	
I want two bottles of beer, three glasses of wine, a pot of green tea.	我要两瓶啤酒，三杯红酒，一壶绿茶。	wǒ yào liǎng píng píjiǔ, sān bēi hóng jiǔ, yī hú lǜ chá.	
Do you like spicy or not spicy?	你要辣的还是不辣的？	nǐ yào là de hái shì bú là de.	
This dish is sweet and sour	这菜又酸又甜。	zhè cài yòu suān yòu tián.	
How is the food/drink?	好吃/喝吗？	hǎo chī / hē ma?	
Delicious (to eat/drink)!	很好/喝吃！	hěn hǎo / hē chī!	

Anything else?	还要别的么？	hái yào bié de me?	
No, that is all.	不用了。	bú yòng le.	
Bill please.	结帐。	jié zhàng.	

Vocabulary

English	Chinese Characters	Pinyin	Notes
To eat/drink	吃/喝	chī/hē	
Menu	菜单	cài dān	
Book a table	定位	dìng wèi	
To order（dish）	点菜	diǎn cài	
Chicken/beef/pork/duck/lamb	鸡肉/牛肉/猪肉/鸭肉/羊肉	jī ròu/niú ròu/zhū ròu/yā ròu/yáng ròu	肉 (ròu) – meat Animals: pig + meat means pork
Egg	鸡/鸭蛋	jī/yā dàn	Chicken/dick egg
Fry/boil/stir fry/steam/BBQ	炸/煮/炒/蒸/烤	zhá/zhǔ/chǎo/zhēng/kǎo	e.g. stir-fried beef is 炒牛肉 (chǎo niú ròu)
Seafood	海鲜	hǎi xiān	
Vegetable/egg	蔬菜/鸡蛋	shū cài/ jī dàn	
Knife/spoon/fork/chopsticks	刀子/勺子/叉子/筷子	dāo zi/sháo zi/chā zi/kuài zi	

Taste	味道	wèi dào	
Rice/noodle/ dumplings	米饭/面条/ 饺子	mǐ fàn / miàn tiáo/ jiǎo zi	
Cola/tea/beer	可乐/茶/啤酒	kě lè / chá /pí jiǔ	
Spicy/sweet/sour	辣/甜/酸	là/tián/suān	
Hard/soft	硬/软	yìng/ruǎn	
Recommend	推荐	tuī jiàn	
Pay	付款	fù kuǎn	
Bill	帐单	zhàng dān	
Delivery	送货	sòng huò	
Take away	外卖	wài mài	
Or	还是	hái shì	
Both.....and....	又….又	yòu…yòu	

- Please 请 (qǐng) is often used at beginning of a sentence.

- An alternative question is one formed of two statements joined by 还是 (háishì) suggesting two different alternatives for the person addressed to choose from.

- 又... 又... means not only but also, used to link to adjectives.

TOPIC 9
TAXIS

English	Chinese Characters	Pinyin	Notes
Hello, where would you like to go?	你好，请问要去哪里？	nǐ hǎo qǐng wèn yào qù nǎ lǐ?	
Please take me to an airport.	请送我到机场。	qǐng sòng wǒ dào jī chǎng.	
Please stop! Wait a minute, I forgot a document.	请停车。等一下，我忘了带文件。	qǐng tíng chē. děng yī xià, wǒ wàngle dài wén jiàn.	
I'd like to pay by cash. Please give me a receipt.	我用现金付款。请给我发票。	wǒ yòng xiàn jīn fù kuǎn. qǐng gěi wǒ fā piào.	发票 (fā piào) is essential for expense claims in China.
Thanks. Please don't forget your belongings.	谢谢。请不要忘记拿你的东西。	xiè xie. qǐng bú yào wàng jì ná nǐ de dōng xi.	

Vocabulary

English	Chinese Characters	Pinyin	Notes
Take a taxi	打车	dǎ chē	
Nearest	最近的	zuì jìn de	
Airport	机场	jī chǎng	

Shopping centre	购物中心	gòu wù zhōng xīn	
Address	地址	dìzhǐ	
Meter	计价器	jì jià qì	
Receipt	发票	fā piào	
Belongings	东西	dōng xi	
Allow	让	ràng	
License number	车牌号码	chē pái hào mǎ	
Stop / parking	停	tíng	

TOPIC 10
COMMUNICATION

English	Chinese Characters	Pinyin	Notes
Sorry, I don't speak Chinese.	对不起，我不会说汉语。	duì bu qǐ wǒ bú huì shuō Hàn yǔ.	
No problem!	没问题！	méi wèn tí!	
I can speak some English.	我能说一些英语。	wǒ néng shuō yì xiē Yīng yǔ.	
Would you mind repeating it? / Could you repeat it please?	你能再说一遍嘛？／请你再说一遍？	nǐ néng zài shūo yí biàn ma?/qǐng nǐ zài shuō yí biàn?	
Could you say it slowly please?	慢点说好吗？	màn diǎn shuō hǎo ma?	
I (listened but) don't understand.	我不明白。	wǒ bù míng bái.	
Can you speak English?	你会说英语吗？	nǐ huì shuō Yīng yǔ ma?	
Can we communicate by email?	我们能用电邮联系吗？	wǒ mén néng yòng diàn yóu lián xì ma?	
Write it down please.	请写下来。	qǐng xiě xià lái.	
"Neng" What does "Neng" means?	"Neng" 是什么意思？	"neng" shì shén mè yì si?	
How do you say "Please" In Chinese?	(请问)我在哪里办理值机手续？	zěn mè yòng Zhōng wén shuō "please"?	

What does "Taitai" mean?	"太太"是什么意思？	"tàitài" shì shénme yì si?	
Are you all right?	你没事吧？你还好吧？	nǐ méi shì ba? nǐ hái hǎo ba?	
Really? Are you joking?	真的吗？你在开玩笑吗？	zhēn de ma? Nǐ zài kāi wán xiào ma?	
What a shame!	太遗憾了！	tài yí hàn le!	
Don't worry!	别着急！	bié zhāo jí!	
Sorry (for a mistake)	抱歉！	bào qiàn!	

Vocabulary

English	Chinese Characters	Pinyin	Notes
Understand	懂/明白	dǒng /míng bái	
Chinese	中文	Zhōng wén	
English	英文	Yīng wén	
French	法文	Fǎwén	
German	德文	Dé wén	
Communicate	交流	jiāo liú	
Great!	太好了	tài hǎo le	
Email address	电子邮箱	diàn zǐ yóu xiāng	
Really	真的	zhēn de	

- The simple complement of degree is usually made of an adjective and the structural particle 得 (de) which is used to connect the verb and its complement of degree.

- The negative form is made by adding a 不 before the complement.

For example:

He speaks French well, but (his) German is not good.
他的法文说得好，但是德文说得不好。
Tā de fǎwén shuō de hǎo, dànshì dé wén shuō dé bù hǎo.

TOPIC 11
MAKING AN APPOINTMENT

English	Chinese Characters	Pinyin	Notes
Are you free at 9:00 tomorrow?	你明天九点有空么？	nǐ míng tiān jiǔ diǎn yǒu kòng me?	
Sorry, I already have appointment then.	对不起，我已经有安排了。	duì bù qǐ, wǒ yǐ jīng yǒu ān pái le.	
What time is good for you?	什么时间方便？	shén mè shí jiān fāng biàn?	
Afternoon, how about 13:00?	中午后，一点什么样？	zhōng wǔ hòu, yī diǎn shén me yàng?	
Meet in the hotel lobby?	我们在酒店大厅见面好吗？	zài Jiǔdiàn dàtīng jiànmiàn hǎo ma?	
Ok, don't be late.	好，别迟到。	hǎo, bié chídào.	
Do not worry, I will arrive early.	不用担心，我会提前到。	bú yòng dān xīn, wǒ huì tí qián dào.	
Sorry, I am late.	对不起，我迟到了。	duì bù qǐ wǒ chí dào le.	

Vocabulary

English	Chinese Characters	Pinyin	Notes
Free	有空	yǒu kòng	
Busy	忙	máng	
Would like	愿意	yuàn yì	
Appointment	约会	yuē huì	
Not available/free	没空	méi kòng	
Convenient	方便	fāng biàn	
Meet	见面	jiàn miàn	
Change (place or time)	换（地点/时间）	huàn(shí jiān /dì diǎn)	
Already	已经	yǐ jīng	

- The verb to have 有 (yǒu) is negated with the particle 没 (méi). The past negative is made by use of 没有 (méi yǒu) instead of 不 (bù). For example,

> I do not have time.
> 我没有空。
> Wǒ méi yǒu kòng.

TOPIC 12
AIRPORTS

English	Chinese Characters	Pinyin	Notes
May I see your passport, please?	请出示你（您）的护照？	qǐng chū shì nǐ (nín) de hù zhào?	您 (nín) The polite and formal form as 你 (nǐ)
This is my passport.	这是我的护照。	zhè shì wǒ de hù zhào.	
Where I can get my baggage (please)?	（请问）我在哪里取行李？	(qǐng wèn) wǒ zài ná lǐ qǔ xíng lǐ?	请问 (qǐng wèn) is a very polite way before you want to ask a question to someone.
I can't find my baggage.	我找不到我的行李了。	wǒ zháo bú dào wǒ de xíng lǐ le.	
Here is my claim tag.	这是我的行李票	zhè shì wǒ de xíng lǐ piào.	
What is my flight number and departure time?	我的航班号和出发时间是多少？	wǒ de háng bān hào hé chū fā shí jīan shì duō shǎo?	
My flight is from Beijing to London.	我的航班是从北京到伦敦的。	wó de háng bān shì cóng Běi jīng dào Lún dūn de.	
Where I can check in?	(请问)我在那里办理值机手续？	(qǐng wèn) wǒ zài ná lǐ bàn lǐ zhí jī shǒu xù?	

| Could you give me a window (aisle) seat? | 能给我一个靠窗户（走廊）的座位嘛？ | néng geǐ wǒ yí gè kào chuāng hù (zǒu láng) de zùo wèi ma? | |
| Where is the taxi stand? | 我在那里能打出租车？ | wǒ zài ná lǐ néng dǎ chū zū chē? | |

Vocabulary

English	Chinese Characters	Pinyin	Notes
Airport	机场	jī chǎng	
Passport	护照	hù zhào	
Baggage	行李	xíng lǐ	
Baggage claim tag	行李票	xíng lǐpiào	
Flight Ticket	飞机票	fēi jī piào	
Flight number	航班号	háng bān hào	
Check in	办理值机	bàn lǐ zhí jī	
Window	窗户	chuāng hù	
Aisle	走廊	zǒu láng	
Beijing	北京	Běi jīng	
London	伦敦	Lún dūn	
Departure	出发	chū fā	

Arrive	到达	dào dá	
See/show something to sb	出示	chū shì	

- 能. . . . . 嘛? Same as "Can" in question sentence.

  For example,

  Can I smoke in the airport?
  我能在机场吸烟嘛？
  Wǒ néng zaì jī chǎng xī yān ma?

  Can you help me to book a fight ticket?
  你能帮我订飞机票嘛？
  Nī néng bāng wǒ dìng fēi jī piào ma?

TOPIC 13
HOTELS

English	Chinese Characters	Pinyin	Notes
Do you have (room) vacancies please?	请问有空房吗？	qǐng wèn yǒu kòng fáng ma?	
May I reserve a single room.	我想预定一个单人房。	wǒ xiǎng yù dìng yī gè dān rén fáng.	
How much for one night?	一个晚上如何收费？	yí gè wǎn shàng rú hé shōu fèi?	
I will stay for three nights.	我住三个晚上。	wǒ zhù sān gè wǎn shàng.	
Do I need pay the deposit?	需要支付定金么？	xū yào zhī fù dìng jīn me?	
I want to change a room.	我想换个房间。	wǒ xiǎng huàn gè fáng jiān.	
Can I access the internet from my room?	能从房间里上网么？	néng cóng fáng jiān lǐ shàng wǎng me?	
Do you have a safe in the room?	房间里有保险柜么？	fáng jiān lǐ yǒu bǎo xiǎn guì me?	
Do you accept credit card?	可以用信用卡付款么？	kě yǐ yòng xìn yòng kǎ fù kuǎn me?	
Please clean the room.	请打扫房间。	qǐng dǎ sǎo fáng jiān.	
I need to check out.	我要退房。	wǒ yào tuì fáng.	

Passport please.	你的护照。	nǐ de hù zhào.	
I want to exchange money.	我想换钱。	wǒ xiǎng huàn qián.	
I'd like to change pounds into RMB.	我想把英镑换成人民币。	wǒ xiǎng bǎ yīng bàng huàn chéng rén mín bì.	
What's the exchange rate today?	今天的汇率是多少?	jīn tiān de huì lǜ shì duō shǎo.	
The rate is 1 pound equals 10.002 RMB.	英镑对人民币一比十点零零二。	yīng bàng duì rén mín bì yī bǐ shí diǎn ling ling èr.	

Vocabulary

English	Chinese Characters	Pinyin	Notes
Free	有空	yǒu kòng	
Reservation	预定	yù dìng	
Single room/ double room/ twin room	单人间/双人间/标准间	dān rén jiān/ shuāng rén jiān/ biāozhǔn jiān	
Check out	退房	tuì fáng	
Not available	空房	kōng fáng	
Baggage	行李	xíng lǐ	
Safe	保险柜	bǎo xiǎng guì	
Towel	毛巾	máo jīn	

Toilet paper/ tissue	卫生纸/纸巾	wèi sheng zhǐ/ zhǐ jīn	
Tooth paste/tooth brush	牙膏/牙刷	yá gāo/yá shuā	
Dryer	吹风机	chuī fēng jī	
Soap	肥皂	féi zào	
Stay	住宿	zhù sù	
Internet	上网	shàng wǎng	
Change(room)	更换（房间）	gēng huàn (fáng jiān)	
Room number	房间号	fáng jiān hào	
Check in	住宿登记	zhù sù dēng jì	
Change (money)	换钱	huàn qián	
Exchange rate	汇率	huì lǜ	
Charge	收费	shōu fèi	
Breakfast/lunch/ dinner	早餐/午餐/ 晚餐	zǎo cān/wǔ cān/ wǎn cān	
Credit card	信用卡	xìn yòng kǎ	
Clean	打扫	dǎ sǎo	
Room	房间	fáng jiān	
Equal	对	duì	
Pound /RMB	英镑/人民币	yīng bàng / rén mín bì	
Passport	护照	hù zhào	

- The preposition 比 (bǐ) may be used to express comparison between two things:

  A 比 **B** adjective + degree

For example,

> My room is larger than yours.
> 我的房间比你的大。
> Wǒ de fángjiān bǐ nǐ de dà.

TOPIC 14
FAMILY MEMBERS

English	Chinese Characters	Pinyin	Notes
I have three children, two sons and a daughter.	我有三个孩子，两个儿子一个女儿。	wǒ yǒusān gè háizi, liǎng gè ér zi yīgè nǚ'ér.	
I don't have brothers but have three older sisters and a younger one.	我没有兄弟（哥哥弟弟），但有三个姐姐一个妹妹。	wǒ méiyǒu xiōngdì (gēge dìdì), dàn yǒusān ge jiějie yīgè mèimei.	
My mother lives in China, my father passed away.	我的母亲住在中国，我的父亲去世了。	wǒ de mǔ qīn zhù zài Zhōng guó, wǒ de fù qīn qù shì le.	
One of my sisters is married. She has one child.	我的姐姐结了婚。她的丈夫是法国人。	wǒ de jiejie jie le hūn. tā de zhàngfū shì Fàguó rén.	

Vocabulary

English	Chinese Characters	Pinyin	Notes
Mother / mum	母亲/妈妈	mǔ qīn / māmā	
Father / dad	父亲/爸爸	fù qīn / bàba	

Older sister	姐姐	jiě jie	
Younger sister	妹妹	mèl mei	
Older brother	哥哥	gē ge	
Younger brother	弟弟	dì di	
Daughter	女儿	nǚ'er	
Son	儿子	ér zi	
Grandmother	奶奶	nǎi nai	
Grandfather	爷爷	yé ye	
Niece	侄女	zhí nǚ	
Nephew	外甥	wài shēng	
Girl	女孩	nǚ hái	
Boy	男孩	nán hái	
Man	男人	nán rén	
Woman	女人	nǚ rén	
Uncle (father's younger brother)	叔叔	shū shu	
Maternal uncle, mother's brother, wife's brother	舅	jiù	
Aunt (mother's sister)	姨	yí	
Aunt, father's sister	姑	gū	

TOPIC 15
THE CHINESE ZODIAC

English	Chinese Characters	Pinyin	Notes
People born under the sign of the Rat are smart, wealthy, hard-working and successful.	属鼠的人, 聪明富有和成功。	shǔ shǔ de rén, cōngmíng fùyǒu hé chénggōng.	
2013 is the Year of the Snake.	二零一三年是蛇年。	èir líng yīsān nián shì shé nián.	
'Fu' character (happiness), combined with a snake twisting around a rabbit as a popular pattern indicating wealth.	剪纸'福'字常用蛇和兔子在一起表示财富。	jiǎn zhǐ fú zì cháng yòng shé hé tù zǐ zài yī qǐ biǎo shì cái fù.	

Vocabulary

English	Chinese Characters	Pinyin	Notes
Rat	鼠	shǔ	
Ox	牛	niú	
Tiger	虎	hǔ	

Rabbit	兔	tù	
Dragon	龙	lóng	
Snake	蛇	shé	
Horse	马	mǎ	
Sheep	羊	yáng	
Monkey	猴	hóuzi	
Rooster	鸡	gōngjī	
Dog	狗	gǒu	
Pig	猪	zhū	

- The 生肖 (Shēng xiāo), better known in English as the Chinese Zodiac, is a scheme that relates each year to animal and its reputed attributes, according to a 12-year mathematical cycle. It has wide currency in several East Asian countries such as China, Vietnam, Korea and Japan.

TOPIC 16
EMERGENCIES

English	Chinese Characters	Pinyin	Notes
Help!	救命！	jiù mìng!	
Danger!	危险！	wēi xiǎn!	
My passport is missing.	我的护照丢了。	wǒ de hù zhào diū le.	
I am lost.	我迷路了。	wǒ mí lù le.	
Can you help me?	能不能帮我一下？	néng bù néng bāng wó yí xià?	
Please help me to call a police.	请帮我叫警察。	qǐng bāng wǒ jiào jǐng chá	
I cannot find my wallet.	我找不到钱包。	wǒ zháo bú dào qiān bāo.	
Can you help me to call an ambulance?	能帮我叫救护车吗？	néng bāng wǒ jiào jiù hù chē ma?	
What's wrong with you?	你怎么了？哪儿不舒服？	nǐ zěn me le？nǎr bù shū fu？	
I've got aheadache.	我头疼。	wǒ tóu téng.	
I am allergic to...	我吃/对。。过敏。	wǒ chī/duì. . . guò mǐn.	
I need to call the police 110.	我要打110。	wǒ yào dǎ yāo-yāo-líng。	
Thief!	小偷！	xiǎo tōu!	

Where is the Toilet / WC / bathroom please?	厕所/洗手间/卫生间/化妆室在哪里？	cè suǒ /xǐ shǒu jiān / wèi shēng jiān / huà zhuāng shì zài nǎ lǐ?	
There was a traffic accident.	出了交通事故。	chū le jiāo tōng shì gù.	
Water is leaking.	漏水了。	lòu shuǐ le.	
Fire!	着火了！	zháo huǒ le.	

Vocabulary

English	Chinese Characters	Pinyin	Notes
Police	警察	jǐng chá	
Raise an alarm /report (an incident) to the police	报警	bào jǐng	
Prohibited / banned	禁止	jìnzhǐ	
Ambulance	救护车	jiù hù chē	
Embassy	大使馆	dā shǐ guǎn	
Passport	护照	hù zhào	
Missing /lost	丢失	diú shī	
Be stolen	被偷	bèi tōu	

Find	找	zhǎo	
Luggage/wallet	行李	xíng lǐ	
Key	钥匙	yào shi	
Emergency exit	紧急出口	jǐn jí chū kōu	exit/entrance/ emergency exit 出口/入口/非常 口 (chūkǒu/rùkǒu/ fēichángkǒu)
Fire extinguisher	灭火器	miè huǒ qì	
Traffic accident	交通事故	jiāo tōng shì gù	
First aid	急救	jí jiù	
Danger	危险	wēi xiǎn	
Help	帮忙	bāng máng	
Leak	漏水	lòu shuǐ	
Fix	修理	xiū lǐ	
Unwell/get sick	不舒服/生病	bù shū fu/shēng bìng	
Medicine	药	yào	
Doctor	医生	yī shēng	
Fever	发烧	fā shāo	
Cough	咳嗽	ké sòu	
Nausea	恶心	ě xīn	
Dizzy	头晕	tóu yūn	

Stomach-ache	肚子疼	dù zi téng	
Allergy	过敏	guò mǐn	

- 我要打 110 (wǒ yào dǎ yāo-yāo-líng). I need to call 110.

  Yāo is an alternate pronunciation for the number one 一 (yī), used because yī is easily confused with seven 七 (qī), especially on the telephone.

- Emergency numbers in China:

  Police: 110
  Fire: 119
  Ambulance: 120

12

POSTSCRIPT

We both hope that you have found our updated analysis of why things happen the way they do in China as useful as we have found them as interesting to peel apart.

Should you have any queries or wish to contact us then please feel free to do so at

www.ukasia.com.cn
or
www.cheltenham-mandarin.co.uk

We wish you every prosperity in your ventures.

APPENDICES

APPENDIX 1

Quick-check chart of important business skills for doing business in China using the ABC Model

1. Artefacts-Focused

Facet/Situation	Core Chinese Issue	Effective Business Response or Preparation
General	*High degree of ritualistic behaviour in much of how Chinese people react to artefacts*	
Ceremonies of welcome and contract signing when National Flags are likely to be seen in far more reverential light than in UK	Confucian respect for order and Face.	Foreign businessmen and women to note PRC national flags with approval or respect and certainly not use as butt for wit. For formal meetings ensure that table top size national flags of PRC are available. Ensure that red and gold PRC flag is never confused with blue, red and white Taiwanese flag.
Business card design	Having both Chinese and English sides gives Face to Chinese culture.	Key tool for initial business contacts.

Facet/Situation	Core Chinese Issue	Effective Business Response or Preparation
Presentation of corporate Gifts on visits to China	As part of highly ritualistic orientation, company cards, logos, and badges assume high importance.	Respect the need for shared identity by having stocks of quality corporate items such as business cards pens and desk ornaments.

2. Behaviour-Focused

Facet/Situation	Core Chinese Issue	Effective Business Response or Preparation
General	*Chinese people remain slightly Group-Oriented*	
Making an appointment	Use 'guanxi' to make initial contact.	More productive.
What to say on meeting Chinese business counterparts	Seeking comfortable social middle ground with others.	Foreign businessmen and women need to master the essential few phrases to show your commitments and gain credibility, although most of their young Chinese counterparts' English will be good.

Facet/Situation	Core Chinese Issue	Effective Business Response or Preparation
How formal does one need to be in China and how does one find out who are the real 'movers and shakers'?	Hierarchy is still a critical issue in all Asians nations regardless of degrees of Westernization and Individualism.	In China it is often difficult to find out who is the most important decision maker in beginning to make up seating plans but prior negotiations between junior staff will normally reveal who is whom.
Will it work if we send our new, highly capable young female MBA to do business in China?	Traditional view of women is changing although some sexist prejudice still exists.	If the young women is fully briefed and empowered she could achieve startlingly successful results.
What do I make of a Chinese SME where the boss is the father and his sons run the organization?	Formality of family responsibilities from Confucius.	In understanding Chinese business associates, recognition of their natural loyalties will assist in working or negotiating with them. Therefore, accept this rather 'Victorian' set up for what it is and work as normal – having found out who really takes the important decisions.

Facet/Situation	Core Chinese Issue	Effective Business Response or Preparation
False Invoices and corruption	Awareness that this Asian tactic is reprehensible in West.	Apply best practice Western ethics for two reasons.
		Firstly, corruption is punishable by death in China and secondly, it is extremely unlikely that a Western businessman or woman will be able to outsmart the Chinese at their own game.
		Therefore, reject such invoices out of hand.
One thing I find unusual with the other side. All the Chinese seem to make all their friends in the company and not at sports clubs, in fact they are very friendly but a bit 'stuffy'.	Friendships should ideally fall in line with family, work and 'senior friend' (Lewis, 1996).	Do not expect to find business counterparts with as wide a range of friends and acquaintances as in the West.
		Therefore, do not expect to make business friendships with same rapidity as in the West but when made will be much longer lasting and mutually beneficial.

3. Communications-Focused

Facet/Situation	Core Chinese Issue	Effective Business Response or Preparation
General	*Highly Formalized language and communications from long literate history*	
What is the best way to communicate with the Chinese? Should we correspond in English or try to do some in Chinese?	High regard for forms of social intercourse.	English is very acceptable in big cities. However, at inland, it is advisable to use both Chinese and English. Write in an easily translatable style i.e. short sentences in which the meaning is exceptionally clear. It is best to have business letters contracts or agreements written in both Chinese and English and which state which language version has primacy in case of any subsequent disagreement. Written Chinese is highly formal and stylized, not just a transcription of the spoken word.

Facet/Situation	Core Chinese Issue	Effective Business Response or Preparation
Company websites	Face demands full introduction of foreign business to Chinese people to avoid uncertainty and move towards Confucian harmony.	Fundamental tool for interested parties to find out more about you and your business and follow up with business contacts. Provide fuller credentials and show your commitment to the China market very clearly. Chinese pages must be designed for Chinese readers and probably much 'busier' in appearance than you would create for the West.
How do we prepare for and proceed in negotiations with the Chinese?	Ethics in Asia are very different from those in the West. Long history of haggling. Signing a contact usually means it is a start of new around of negotiation.	Essential to prepare for negotiations in far greater depth than would be normal in West. Expect delays, obfuscation, constant referrals back to higher authority and minute changes as well as the treating of any signed contract as merely basis for further change.
I have this uneasy feeling that what actually happened and was agreed to is being reinterpreted, and not always to our best interest.	Business is built on mutual trust between individuals rather than institutions. Truth itself is a complex issue.	Businessmen and women from specific Western culture need to be aware of diffuse view of Truth and so need to probe and confirm constantly to be certain that both sides are of one mind.

Facet/Situation	Core Chinese Issue	Effective Business Response or Preparation
We have worked our way through some pretty tough negotiations and when I was insulted and replied in kind everything went very, very quiet. What happened?	Face. Also silence is part of vocabulary in Chinese to give people a chance to reflect and think.	Central to the Chinese character is the concept of 'Face' or mianzi. It is a highly complex issue but is in essence associated to the maintenance of personal dignity and Confucian harmony. Personal slights are taken very seriously, seldom forgiven and never forgotten. Avoid direct questions, which may humiliate the Chinese into by admitting inability or giving a false answer to appease. Avoid direct or public criticism. Pose hard questions by including a 'get out' clause so that you retain control of discussion and do not lose the sense in cross-cultural exchanges. Do allow a brief silences between your negotiation or conversation as that is how Chinese people communicate.

Facet/Situation	Core Chinese Issue	Effective Business Response or Preparation
Is it worth my while learning any Chinese for business.	Recognition of limitations of using only mother tongues for trade.	At least, learn some simple greetings and a few polite phrases of Chinese for meetings and social events – they will be very well received and you will be taken more seriously. Through learning a new language you will gain insight of a new culture and the people. Making far better business decisions as a result. If you learn some Chinese, you will be able to judge if an interpreter is competent and whether they fully understand your business and whether they can be trusted to translate fully in both directions.
We signed a contract after long hard negotiations and now the Chinese insist on changing it bit by bit. What are they doing?	Awareness that West do not share Oriental view on fluidity of points of agreement embarrasses younger Western trained businessmen and women but their elders do not see matters that way.	Central Government is working hard to put a credible legal framework in place and so one can be robust and insist on individual companies abiding by their written agreements and make this clear as contract negotiations proceed. Recourse to local government or press can work wonders.

APPENDIX 2
ABC Model questionnaires

UK business example

The questionnaires presented to the samples of approximately 50 UK and 50 Chinese businessmen and women from different locations between the ages of 24 and 56 years old were designed to be identical – apart from the languages used – to draw out indicative data to enable practical inter-cultural conclusions to be drawn. The Artefacts, Behaviours and Communications questionnaires now follow, the mean scores being underlined.

1. Artefacts

10 = I totally agree, 1 = I totally disagree, 0 = No response

	Question	Score
1.	A national flag is the most important symbol of a nation.	0 1 2 3 4 5 **6** 7 8 9 10
2.	The framework of a nation's government is essential to any country.	0 1 2 3 **4** 5 6 7 8 **9** 10
3.	Emblems and badges fully support national culture.	0 1 2 3 4 5 **6** 7 8 9 10
4.	Uniforms support national culture.	0 1 2 3 4 5 **6** 7 8 9 10
5.	The way our companies do business is a good indication of our national culture.	0 1 2 3 4 5 6 **7** 8 9 10
6.	The way we dress shows the rest of the world how we see ourselves.	0 1 2 3 4 5 6 7 **8** 9 10
7.	A company song is essential to the success of our company.	0 1 2 3 **4** 5 6 7 8 9 10
8.	I look forward very much to receiving company pins in recognition of my service.	0 1 2 3 **4** 5 6 7 8 9 10

| 9. | Senior managers merit a driver for their company car | 0 1 2 3 **4** 5 6 7 8 9 10 |
| 10. | Visits by important political, industrial or foreign visitors must be marked by an exchange of gifts. | 0 1 2 3 **4** 5 6 7 8 9 10 |

2. Behaviours

10 = I totally agree, 1 = I totally disagree, 0 = No response

	Question	**Score**
1.	It is important to attend company social events after working hours.	0 1 2 3 4 5 **6** 7 8 9 10
2.	All my friends have come from my company	0 1 2 3 **4** 5 6 7 8 9 10
3.	In my company we have a special dress code (colour and style of suits, shirts/blouses, etc)	0 1 2 3 **4** 5 6 7 8 9 10
4.	It is not important to have friends and acquaintances that do not work for my company.	0 1 2 **3** 4 5 6 7 8 9 10
5.	We all say 'good morning' in the same way when we get to work.	0 1 2 3 4 5 **6** 7 8 9 10
6.	We all respect each other's personal space.	0 1 2 3 4 5 **6** 7 8 9 10
7.	Meals at work are very important.	0 1 2 3 **4** 5 6 7 8 9 10
8.	Early-morning exercise makes us all a more powerful force.	0 1 2 **3** 4 5 6 7 8 9 10
9.	Business cards are important and one must receive them properly and read them carefully	0 1 2 **3** 4 5 6 7 8 9 10
10.	Foreign businessmen should be treated as openly as possible.	0 1 2 3 **4** 5 6 7 8 9 10
11.	Foreign businesswomen should be treated exactly the same as foreign businessmen.	0 1 2 3 4 5 **6** 7 8 9 10
12.	I would always ask a foreign business visitor about his family.	0 1 2 3 4 5 **6** 7 8 9 10
13.	I would always let a foreign business visitor know the details of my family life.	0 1 2 3 **4** 5 6 7 8 9 10

14.	I would not respect a foreign national being untidily dressed.	0 1 2 3 4 5 6 **7** 8 9 10
15.	It is very important that during meals people are placed in an appropriate seat according to their status.	0 1 2 3 4 5 **6** 7 8 9 10
16.	It makes good business sense to issue dummy invoices to speed negotiations.	0 1 **2 3** 4 5 6 7 8 9 10
17.	The arrangement of seats for business meetings is critical to the success of the meeting.	0 1 2 3 4 **5** 6 7 8 9 10
18.	For many employees the traditional pattern of loyalty to one's employer is a thing of the past.	0 1 2 3 4 5 **6** 7 8 9 20
19.	Whenever business colleagues meet together outside working hours and outside the workplace it's for pleasure and not because they feel obliged to out of a sense of duty.	0 1 2 3 **4** 5 6 7 8 9 10
20.	Managers are strongly in favour of encouraging individual effort, especially when it involves dynamic young executives who want 'to get on' and 'make their mark'.	0 1 2 3 4 **5** 6 7 8 910
21.	People don't seem to have the same sense of social obligation to each other (like trying to persuade one's manager to employ one's cousin) as they do in some countries, like India for example.	0 1 2 3 4 5 **6** 7 8 9 10
22.	Most prominent executives have no concept of social disgrace, shame or loss of face if things go wrong in their business affairs.	0 1 2 3 4 5 6 **7** 8 9 10
23.	Promotion at work is based more on merit than on seniority	0 1 2 3 4 **5** 6 7 8 9 10
24.	Success in business, and in management too, seems to depend more on how competitive you are and not how caring.	0 1 2 3 4 5 6 7 **8** 9 10
25.	People generally like foreign visitors, provided they do not simply try to impose their ways of doing things.	0 1 2 3 4 5 **6** 7 8 9 10

3. Communications

10 = I totally agree, 1 = I totally disagree, 0 = No response

	Question	Score
1.	Good manners between people are very important.	0 1 2 3 4 **5** 6 7 8 9 10
2.	The correct way to write letters is an important business skill.	0 1 2 3 4 **5** 6 7 8 9 10
3.	Negotiating skills are essential to business.	0 1 2 3 4 5 6 **7** 8 9 10
4.	It is important to recognise that business agreements are dynamic.	0 1 2 3 4 **5** 6 7 8 9 10
5.	The boss is always right.	0 1 2 3 4 **5** 6 7 8 9 10
6.	Women have equal ability in the workplace.	0 1 2 3 4 5 **6** 7 8 9 10
7.	It is only appropriate that one finds a good job for family relations.	0 1 2 3 **4** 5 6 7 8 9 10
8.	The family is more important than anything else.	0 1 2 3 4 5 **6** 7 8 9 10
9.	Truth is a complex issue.	0 1 2 3 4 5 **6** 7 8 9 10
10.	One should always avoid causing offence in discussion.	0 1 2 3 **4** 5 6 7 8 9 10
11.	It is important in business to speak foreign languages.	0 1 2 3 **4** 5 6 7 8 9 10
12.	Interpreters can be relied upon to handle all language issues in meetings allowing business people to concentrate on business.	0 1 2 3 4 5 **6** 7 8 9 10
13.	Business people are typically very straightforward, explicit, quick and direct in how they communicate, even in negotiations.	0 1 2 3 **4** 5 6 7 8 9 10
14.	It is only sensible to use guile in negotiation.	0 1 2 3 4 5 6 7 8 9 10

Chinese business example

1. Artefacts

"十" 表示 "我完全同意"
"零" 表示 "我完全不同意"
10 = I totally agree, 1 = I totally disagree, 0 = No response

	问题	
	Question	**Score**
一	国旗是一个国家最重要的标志	零一二三四五六七八九十
1.	A national flag is the most important symbol of a nation.	0 1 2 3 4 5 6 7 8 <u>9</u> 10
二	国家的政府是任何国家必不可少的机关。	零一二三四五六七八九十
2.	The framework of a nation's government is essential to any country.	0 1 2 3 4 5 6 7 <u>8</u> 9 10
三	象征和徽章完全支持国家文化。	零一二三四五六七八九十
3.	Emblems and badges fully support national culture.	0 1 2 3 4 5 6 7 <u>8</u> 9 10
四	制服表现一个国家文化。	零一二三四五六七八九十
4.	Uniforms support national culture.	0 1 2 3 4 <u>5</u> 6 7 8 9 10
五	我们中国公司作贸易的方法表达着我国的文化。	零一二三四五六七八九十
5.	The way our companies do business is a good indication of our national culture.	0 1 2 3 4 <u>5</u> 6 7 8 9 10
六	中国人的穿着是让世界了解我们怎么样看自己的外貌。	零一二三四五六七八九十
6.	The way we dress shows the rest of the world how we see ourselves.	0 1 2 3 4 5 6 <u>7</u> 8 9 10
七	一个公司歌或校歌对于公司或学校的成功至关重要。	零一二三四五六七八九十
7.	A company or school song is essential to the success of our school or company.	0 1 2 3 4 <u>5</u> 6 7 8 9 10

八	我特别盼望接收到奖章或荣誉证书作为我为公服务的认可。	零一二三四五六七八九十
8.	I look forward very much to receiving company pins in recognition of my service.	0 1 2 3 4 5 <u>6</u> 7 8 9 10
九	每一位高阶层的管理人员值得配备司机及高级车。	零一二三四五六七八九十
9.	Senior managers merit a driver for their company car.	0 1 2 3 4 5 <u>6</u> 7 8 9 10
十	重要人物访问时应该送礼物。	零一二三四五六七八九十
10.	Visits by important political, industrial or foreign visitors must be marked by an exchange of gifts.	0 1 2 3 4 5 <u>6</u> 7 8 9 10

2. Behaviours

10 = I totally agree, 1 = I totally disagree, 0 = No response

	Question	Score
一	参加班后的酒会酒筵等社交活动对工作很重要。	零一二三四五六七八九十
1.	It is important to attend company social events after working hours.	0 1 2 3 4 5 <u>6</u> 7 8 9 10
二	我的朋友都是我公司的同事。	零一二三四五六七八九十
2.	All my friends have come from my company.	0 1 <u>2</u> 3 4 5 6 7 8 9 10
三	在公司，我们须穿正装（颜色，式样等）	零一二三四五六七八九十
3.	In my company we have a special dress code (colour and style of suits, shirts/blouses, etc)	0 1 2 3 <u>4</u> 5 6 7 8 9 10
四	我公司外的朋友没有公司里的那么重要。	零一二三四五六七八九十
4.	It is not important to have friends and acquaintances that do not work for my company.	<u>0</u> 1 2 3 4 5 6 7 8 9 10
五	上班时我们和同事在早上问好时用标准的说法。	零一二三四五六七八九十

5.	We all say 'good morning' in the same way when we get to work.	0 1 2 3 4 5 6 7 <u>8</u> 9 10
六	我们尊重他人的私生活和空间。	零一二三四五六七八九十
6.	We all respect each other's personal space.	0 1 2 3 4 <u>5</u> 6 7 8 9 10
七	在公司和同事在一起吃饭非常重要。	零一二三四五六七八九十
7.	Meals at work are very important.	0 1 2 3 <u>4</u> 5 6 7 8 9 10
八	早晨作运动能使我们工作组更强壮，也更有效率。	零一二三四五六七八九十
8.	Early-morning exercise makes us all a more powerful force.	0 1 2 3 4 <u>5</u> 6 7 8 9 10
九	因为名片对工作很重要，所以接受名片和给名片礼节非常重要。	零一二三四五六七八九十
9.	Business cards are important and one must receive them properly and read them carefully.	0 1 2 3 4 5 6 7 <u>8</u> 9 10
十	我们应该公开和平等地和外商沟通。	零一二三四五六七八九十
10.	Foreign businessmen should be treated as openly as possible.	0 1 2 3 4 5 6 7 <u>8</u> 9 10
十一	对女外商我们应该像对待男外商一样平等。	零一二三四五六七八九十
11.	Foreign businesswomen should be treated exactly the same as foreign businessmen.	0 1 2 3 4 5 6 7 8 <u>9</u> 10
十二	谈生意时我会问侯外商的家人。	零一二三四五六七八九十
12.	I would always ask about a visiting business visitor about his family.	0 1 2 3 4 <u>5</u> 6 7 8 9 10
十三	谈生意时我会向外商介绍我的家人情况。	零一二三四五六七八九十
13.	I would always let a foreign business visitor know the details of my family life.	0 1 <u>2</u> 3 4 5 6 7 8 9 10
十四	我对不穿正装或穿着不当的外商没有好印象。	零一二三四五六七八九十
14.	I would not respect a visiting businessperson being untidily dressed.	0 1 2 3 4 <u>5</u> 6 7 8 9 10

十五	酒筵时座位要看每个人的地位。	零一二三四五六七八九十
15.	It is very important that during meals people are placed in an appropriate seat according to their status.	0 1 2 3 4 5 6 7 <u>8</u> 9 10
十六	去加速谈判用假发票。	零一二三四五六七八九十
16.	It makes good business sense to issue dummy invoices to speed negotiations.	0 1 2 3 4 <u>5</u> 6 7 8 9 10
十七	谈生意的关键在于谈生意时每家客商的座位。	零一二三四五六七八九十
17.	The arrangement of seats for business meetings is critical to the success of the meeting.	0 1 2 3 <u>4</u> 5 6 7 8 9 10
十八	经理们都支持个人发展,特别是让年青有才华的人发挥自己的才能。	零一二三四五六七八九十
18.	For many employees the traditional pattern of loyalty to one's employer is a thing of the past.	0 1 2 3 4 <u>5</u> 6 7 8 9 10
十九	下班后同事会面是因为他们喜欢在一起，不是因为受上司的压力。	零一二三四五六七八九十
19.	Whenever business colleagues meet together outside working hours and outside the workplace it's for pleasure and not because they feel obliged to out of a sense of duty.	0 1 2 3 4 5 6 <u>7</u> 8 9 10
二十	经理们都支持个人，特别是年青有才华的人发挥自己的才能。	零一二三四五六七八九十
20.	Managers are strongly in favour of encouraging individual effort, especially when it involves dynamic young executives who want to "get on" and "make their mark".	0 1 2 3 4 5 6 <u>7</u> 8 9 10
二十一	除了印度之外，别的国家好像没有雇用家人或亲属族的义务和习惯。	零一二三四五六七八九十
21.	People don't seem to have the same sense of social obligation to each other (like trying to persuade one's manger to employ one's cousin) as they seem to have in some countries, like India for example.	0 1 2 <u>3</u> 4 5 6 7 8 9 10

二十二	如果公司管理不好或项目失败，很多公司管理人员没有丢面子，没脸见人的概念。	零一二三四五六七八九十
22.	Most company executives have no concept of social disgrace, shame or loss of face if things go wrong in their business affairs.	0 1 2 3 4 <u>5</u> 6 7 8 9 10
二十三	很多公司的晋级制度是按能力，不是按资历。	零一二三四五六七八九十
23.	Promotion at work is based more on merit than on seniority	0 1 2 3 4 <u>5</u> 6 7 8 9 10
二十四	在事业和管理上要成功，是看你的竞争力，不是看你人好不好。	零一二三四五六七八九十
24.	Success in business, and in management too, seems to depend more on how competitive you are and not how caring.	0 1 2 3 4 5 <u>6</u> 7 8 9 10
二十五	一般来说，人们喜欢外商，如果他们能尊重我国的文化。	零一二三四五六七八九十
25.	People generally like foreign investors, provided they do not simply try to impose their ways of doing things.	0 1 2 3 4 5 <u>6</u> 7 8 9 10

3. Communications

10 = I totally agree, 1 = I totally disagree, 0 = No response

	Question	Score
一	对于人际关系，礼节非常重要。	零一二三四五六七八九十
1.	Good manners between people are very important.	0 1 2 3 4 5 <u>6</u> 7 8 9 10
二	能正确地写商业信是一种重要商业工作能力。	零一二三四五六七八九十
2.	The correct way to write letters is an important business skill.	0 1 2 3 4 5 6 7 8 <u>9</u> 10
三	商业谈判能力是商业工作的关键能力。	零一二三四五六七八九十
3.	Negotiating skills are essential to business.	0 1 2 3 4 5 6 7 <u>8</u> 9 10
四	我们都须了解商业协议会常常改变。	零一二三四五六七八九十
4.	It is important to recognise that business agreements are dynamic.	0 1 2 3 4 5 6 7 <u>8</u> 9 10
五	老板总是正确的。	零一二三四五六七八九十
5.	The boss is always right.	0 1 2 3 <u>4</u> 5 6 7 8 9 10
六	在工作中女人跟男人的能力是一样的。	零一二三四五六七八九十
6.	Women have equal ability in the workplace.	0 1 2 3 4 5 6 7 <u>8</u> 9 10
七	帮助家属找工作没有什么不合适。	零一二三四五六七八九十
7.	It is only appropriate that one finds a good job for family relations.	0 1 2 3 <u>4</u> 5 6 7 8 9 10
八	照顾家人是最重要的。	零一二三四五六七八九十
8.	The family is more important than anything else.	0 1 2 3 4 5 6 <u>7</u> 8 9 10
九	真理是非常复杂的问题。	零一二三四五六七八九十
9.	Truth is a complex issue.	0 1 2 3 4 5 6 7 <u>8</u> 9 10

十	谈话时一定不要得罪人。	零一二三四五六七八九十
10.	One should always avoid causing offence in discussion.	0 1 2 3 4 5 6 7 <u>8</u> 9 10
十一	懂外语对于商业工作非常重要。	零一二三四五六七八九十
11.	It is important in business to speak foreign languages.	0 1 2 3 4 5 6 7 8 <u>9</u> 10
十二	商人在谈判时谈生意，让翻译执行翻译工作。	零一二三四五六七八九十
12.	Interpreters can be relied upon to handle all language issues in meetings allowing business people to concentrate on business.	0 1 2 3 4 5 6 7 8 <u>9</u> 10
十三	一般商人在谈判时会直截了当，一针见血。	零一二三四五六七八九十
13.	Business people are typically very straightforward, explicit, quick and direct in how they communicate, even in negotiations.	0 1 2 3 4 5 <u>6</u> 7 8 9 10
十四	谈判时用不同的策略是很明智的。	零一二三四五六七八九十
14.	It is only sensible to use guile in negotiation.	0 1 2 3 4 <u>5</u> 6 7 8 9 10

APPENDIX 3
Special industrial areas and zones in China

Special Economic Zone (SEZ)

SEZs were set up following an initiative by Deng Xiaoping in 1979 and created the first window China opened to the outside world. Originally they were the experimental arena for China's economic reform and open-door policy

- 5+1: Shenzhen, Zhuhai, Shantou, Xiamen, Hainan Island, and Shanghai Pudong – all in the coastal area
- Special policies and incentives (duty-free, tax breaks, etc) granted at early stage, not many at present
- 15% corporate income tax rate for all enterprises, compared to the rate of 33% in most parts of China
- Shanghai Pudong and Shenzhen emerged as China's international cities

Economic & Technological Development Zone (ETDZ)

- National certified, located in major industrial and commercial cities across the country
- Pioneering zones in the region with good infrastructure to facilitate foreign investment
- Focus on manufacturing labour-intensive consumer products
- Foreign investors aiming at China market entry or lowering cost of export
- Many other local ETDZs, not nationally-certified, less regulated, not recommended

Free Trade Zone (FTZ)

- Enclosed, bonded zones
- Sited along coastal area and in cities with port facilities
- Function: transit trading, distribution, logistics services, and manufacturing
- FTZs also enjoy the same policies and incentives as ETDZs.
- Import license free
- Duty free/bonded for all imported goods (manufacturing and office equipment, components, etc)
  - No VAT in the zone
  - Simplified customs clearance procedures
  - No customs fee for storage and transit goods
  - Less foreign exchange control

High-Tech Park

- Focus on new and advanced technologies
- Function: technology products manufacturing, R&D, start-up and education
- Parks in parks: Incubator Campus, Software Park, IC Design Park, Overseas Returnees Park, etc
- Home for the China high-tech big companies like Huawei, Lenovo, SMIC, ZTE, etc
- Pool of international and local venture capitals
- Besides the same policies and incentives as ETDZs, High-Tech Park also enjoy:
  - Local government subsidized land price and property rental
  - Central and local government funding support
  - VAT subsidies

Export Processing Zone (EPZ)

- Mostly located in ETDZs
- Enclosed, bonded zones
- Function: manufacturing for export only
- Besides the same policies and incentives as ETDZs, EPZ also enjoy:
  - Import license free

– Duty free/bonded for all imported goods
– No VAT in the zone
– Goods (including public utilities) export to EPZ from China qualified for VAT rebate
– Simplified customs clearance procedures, 24/7 schedule
– Less foreign exchange control

Bonded Logistics Zone (BLZ)

- BLZ: Shanghai, Shenzhen, Dalian, Tianjin, Qingdao, Zhangjiagang, Ningbo, and Xiamen. All connect to ports, so called "Zone-Port Connection"
- Bonded Logistics Centre (Type B): Suzhou
- Function: bonded warehousing, international distribution/delivery, simple processing & value-added service, transit trading, and virtual port
- Incentives:
  - Goods from overseas are bonded, no customs duty or VAT required
  - Goods from China are regarded as exports and enjoy VAT rebate when entering BLZ
  - Goods in BLZ are allowed to consolidate, transfer and store without time limit

APPENDIX 4
Auspicious/inauspicious numbers?
What numbers?

The number 3, 三 (sān), sounds like 生 (shēng) which in Mandarin means birth; a new life is always welcomed in China.

The number 5, 五 (wǔ), is associated with the five elemental guardians: Water, Fire, Earth, Wood, and Metal in Chinese philosophy, and in turn historically associated with the Emperor of China. For example, the Tiananmen gate, being the main thoroughfare to the Forbidden City, has five arches.

The number 6, 六 (liù), sounds like the homophone for blessings, happiness, prosperity 禄 (lù). It also sounds like 溜 (liù) a swift current and 流 (liú) ,fluid, and is considered good for business.

The number 7, 七 (qī), symbolises "togetherness". It sounds like 起 (qǐ) meaning to rise, to launch or to establish.

The number 8, 八 (bā), is really lucky as it sounds similar to 发 (fā), short for 发财 (fācái) means to get rich, prosper or wealth. For example, the opening ceremony of the Summer Olympics in Beijing began at 8 seconds and 8 minutes past 8 pm on 8th August 2008, the United Airlines route from San Francisco to Beijing is Flight UA88 and a Commerce Bank branch in New York's Chinatown raffled off Safety Deposit Box No. 888 for a huge amount of money in view of the prosperity and good fortune it would bring its owner.

Number 9, 九 (jiǔ), sounds the same as 久 meaning "long-lasting", often used in weddings. The Emperor's robes often had nine dragons and Chinese mythology held that the dragon always had nine children.

The number 4, 四 (sì) in Chinese, Korean, and Japanese has a similar sound as 死 (sǐ), death and is not regarded as lucky at all. Most people try their best to avoid not associate with the number. For example, Nokia Mobil phones have no series beginning with a 4 and in East Asia, there is no 4th or 14th, 24th floor in many high rise buildings.

The Chinese have a saying that good things come in pairs and so use double symbols in product brand names – for example 喜 (xǐ) meaning joy or happiness, may be extended to 囍 (shuāng xǐ), meaning double happiness.

BIBLIOGRAPHY

Ames, R, *The Art of Warfare*, Random House, 1993

August, O, *Chinese high-flyer has no time for the party*, The Times, 1 May 2002

http://www.business-anti-corruption.com/en/country-profiles/east-asia-the-pacific/china/snapshot/

http://www.immi.se/intercultural/nr19/tianbo.htm

Chan, W-T A, *Source Book in Chinese Philosophy*, Princeton University Press, 1963

http://chinadivide.com 2012

China Insurance Regulatory Commission, *http://www .circ .gov .cn*

Chung, C, *An Outline of Chinese Geography*, Foreign Languages Press, Peking, 1978

Chuang, T, *Mystic, Moralist, and Social Reformer*, Kelly & Walsh, Shanghai, AMS Press, New York, 1968

Clavell, J, *The Art of War*, Delacorte Press, 1983

Cleary, T, *The Art Of War* , Shambhala Publications, 1991

Cleary, T, *The Essential Tao: An Initiation into the Heart of Taoism Through the Authentic Tao Te Ching and the Inner Teachings of Chuang-Tzu*, 1992

Clifford, P, 'Beyond the Sofa Factor', *The Wall Street Journal*, 24 August 2005

http://commons.wikimedia.org/wiki/File:Population_density_of_China_by_first-level_administrative_regions(English).png

Cotterell, A, *China. A History*, Pimlico, London,1988

Dana, L. P., 'Culture is of the essence in Asia', *Mastering Management, Financial Times*, 27 November 2000, pp 12-13

DeNoble, D, *Former Kro's Nest manager blogged about the situation in 2010*, http://chinadivide.com, 11 May 2010

The Art of War: the Denma translation, Shambhala Publications, 2001

Evans-Smith, W, *China, A Country Study*, Foreign Area Studies, The American University, Third Edition, Washington DC, 1981

Fang, F, *China Fever*, 2007

Feng, GF and English, J C , *Inner Chapters*, Vintage Books, New York, 1974

Fenby, J, *Big Money in Modern China,* The Sunday Times Magazine, 17 October 2004

Gao, LL, *Taking a Stand*, The China Business Review, November-December 1994

Gagliardi, G, *The Art of War and The Ancient Chinese Revealed*, Clearbridge Publishing, Hillsborough, Washington, 2003

Garrison, T, *International Business Culture*, Third Edition, ELM Publications, Huntingdon, 2001

Gelder, P van, *Bridging the Gap between Necessity and Resistance: Theoretical Frameworks For Methodology and Learning in Cross-Cultural Training*, Amsterdam, 2008

Giles, H A, *The Sacred Books of China: The Texts of Taoism*, Part I,Kelly and Walsh, 1926

Global Business Culture, *Business Culture in the UK*, www.eprogrammes.com

http://www.blplaw.com/download/China_Legal_update_-_China_adjusts_its_foreign_investment_guidelines.pdf

http://www.globalprofitsalert.com/china-stock-digest/a-million-new-millionaires-what-are-they-buying-118541, 5 Mar 11

Gonzalez-Carrasco, C A , *Reframing Complexity in International leadership and management*, SIETAR EUROPE, York University, September 18, 2009

http://www.youtube.com/watch?v=oiwMiuGJE6w

Graham, A C, *Philosophical Argument in Ancient China*, 1993

Graham, A C, *Chuang Tzu: The Seven Inner Chapters and other writings from the book 'Chuang-tzu'*, George Allen & Unwin, London, 2001

Griffith, S B, *The Art of War*, Oxford University Press, 1963

Guisso RWL, Pagani C, and Miller D, *The First Emperor of China*, 1989 Sidgwick and Jackson, London

Henley Management College, *Inter- Cultural Management – Workbook*, Henley-on-Thames, 1997

Hiscock, G, *Asia's New Wealth Club*, Nicholas Brealey Publishing, London 2000

http://history.howstuffworks.com/asian-history/history-of-china6.htm

Hofstede, G, *Culture's Consequences*, Second Edition, Sage Publications, Thousand Oaks, 2001

Hofstede, G, *Cultures and Organizations*, Profile Books Ltd, London, 2003

Hu, HY and Feng, ZW, *Da Vinci Code to success*, China Daily 21 August 2012

Huang, J H, *The Art of War: The New Translation*, Quill William Morrow, 1993

Huang R, *1587 A Year of No Significance: The Ming Dynasty in Decline*, Yale University Press, New Haven, CT, 1981

Hucker, C O, *China to 1850, A Short History*, Stanford University Press, Stanford,1978

Hutchings, G, *Modern China A Companion to a Rising Power*, Penguin Books, Harmondsworth, 2000

Huynh, T, *The Art of War: Spirituality for Conflict*, Skylight Paths Publishing, 2008

http://www.jincao.com/fa/24/law24.htm

Kaufman, S F, *The Art of War: The Definitive Interpretation of Sun Tzu's Classic Book of Strategy*, Tuttle Publishing, 1996

Krause, D G, *The Art of War For Executives*, Perigee Books, 1995

Kruger, R, *All Under Heaven. A complete history of China*, John Wiley & Sons, Chichester, 2003

Leonhardt, D, *The Real Problem With China*, The New York Times, 11 January 2011

Lewis, R D, *Cross-Cultural Communication, A Visual Approach*, Transcreen Publications, Warnford, 2008

Lewis, R D, *When Cultures Collide, Managing Successfully Across Cultures*, Nicholas Brealey Publishing, London ,2001

Mackay, A and Tatham, S, *Behavioural Conflict from General to Strategic Corporal: Complexity, Adaptation and Influence*, The Shrivenham Papers Number 9, The Defence Academy of The United Kingdom, Shrivenham, December 2009

Mair, V H, *The Art of War: Sun Zi's Military Methods*, Columbia University Press, 2007

Minford, J, *The Art of War*, Viking, 2002

National Centre for Social Research, *British Social Attitudes 26th Report*, London, 2010

National Centre for Social Research, *British Social Attitudes 25th Report*, London, 2009

The New York Times *'The Real Problem With China'* 11 Jan 2011

The Patent Office of The People's Republic of China, http://www.cpo.cn.net/

http://www.circ.gov.cn

Petrie, M, *Cross-cultural Analysis: A Focus on Chinese and British Business Behaviour Patterns*, Henley Management College, 2003

Petrie, M J, *Talking with the New Business Dragons*, Management Books 2000, Kemble, 2005

PricewaterhouseCoopers, *Selling in China: Moving Beyond the "Sofa Factor"*

Pucik, V., Tichy, N. M. and Barnett, C. K., *Globalising Management*, John Wiley & Sons Inc., New York, 1992

Rees, D, *Human Resources 'Due Diligence'*, 2000

Rees, D, *Managing Culture*, 1999

Said, E W, *Culture and Imperialism*, Chatto & Windus, London, 1993

Shun, K L, *Mencius*, The Stanford Encyclopedia of Philosophy, 2012

Spence J D, *Emperor of China: Self Portrait of Kang-Hsi*, Vintage Books, New York, 1974

http://www.stats.gov.cn/zgrkpc/dlc/

Sun, T, *The Art of War by – Special Edition*, El Paso Norte Press, 2005

Sun, T, *The Art of War*, translated and annotated by Ralph D. Sawyer, Barnes & Noble 1994

Sun, Z, *Art of War: An Illustrated Translation with Asian Perspectives and Insights*, Pearson Education Asia, 2003

http://www.tradingeconomics.com/china/imports

Trippon, J, *A Million New Millionaires – what are they buying?* Global Profit Alert, 5 March 2011

http://www.transparency.org.uk/our-work/publications/95-adequate-procedures--- guidance-to-the-uk-bribery-act-2010

UK Bribery Act 2010, *http://www.justice.gov.uk/legislation/bribery*

UNICEF – China – Statistics – *www.unicef.org/infobycountry/china_statistics.html*

Ed. Velasquez, J, Yoshiro, M, Yoshimira, S, Ono, I, *Innovative Communities: People-centred Approaches to Environmental Management in the Asia-Pacific Region*, UN University Press, Tokyo, 2005

Ware, James R, *The Sayings of Chuang Chou*. New York: Mentor Classics, 1963

Watson, Burton, *The Complete Works of Chuang Tzu*. New York: Columbia University Press 1968. ISBN 978-0-231-03147-9

http://en.wikipedia.org/wiki/Confucius

http://en.wikipedia.org/wiki/Wu_Xing

Wing, RL, Sun Tzu translated and annotated *The Art of Strategy*. Main Street Books

1988

Xu, ZL, and Nong Z, *National Bureau of Statistics* 2009-2010 report

Yap, Y and Cotterell, A, *Chinese Civilization*, George Weidenfeld and Nicholson, London, 1977

Yuan, S B, *Sun Tzu's Art of War: The Modern Chinese Interpretation*, Sterling Publishing Co., Inc, 1987

INDEX